LEADERSHIP FOR FAMILY AND COMMUNITY INVOLVEMENT

The Soul of Educational Leadership

ALAN M. BLANKSTEIN, PAUL D. HOUSTON, ROBERT W. COLE, EDITORS

THE SOUL OF EDUCATIONAL LEADERSHIP

VOLUME 8

———— ❧ ————

LEADERSHIP FOR FAMILY AND COMMUNITY INVOLVEMENT

———— ❧ ————

PAUL D. HOUSTON ❧ ALAN M. BLANKSTEIN ❧ ROBERT W. COLE

EDITORS

A JOINT PUBLICATION

CORWIN PRESS
A SAGE Company
Thousand Oaks, CA 91320

For information:

Corwin
A SAGE Company
2455 Teller Road
Thousand Oaks, California 91320
(800) 233-9936
Fax: (800) 417-2466
www.corwin.com

SAGE Ltd.
1 Oliver's Yard
55 City Road
London EC1Y 1SP
United Kingdom

SAGE India Pvt. Ltd.
B 1/I 1 Mohan Cooperative
Industrial Area
Mathura Road, New Delhi 110 044
India

SAGE Asia-Pacific Pte. Ltd.
33 Pekin Street #02-01
Far East Square
Singapore 048763

Printed in the United States of America

Library of Congress Cataloging-in-Publication Data

Leadership for family and community involvement/Paul D. Houston, Alan M. Blankstein, Robert W. Cole, editors; A Joint Publication with HOPE Foundation and the American Association of School Administrators
    p. cm.—(The soul of educational leadership; v. 8)
Includes bibliographical references and index.
ISBN 978-1-4129-8127-9 (pbk.)

1. Education—Parent participation. 2. Community and school. 3. Educational leadership. I. Houston, Paul D. II. Blankstein, Alan M., 1959- III. Cole, Robert W., 1945- IV. Title. V. Series.

LB1048.5.L43 2010
371.19'2—dc22   2010011773

This book is printed on acid-free paper.

10   11   12   13   14   10   9   8   7   6   5   4   3   2   1

Acquisitions Editor:	Arnis Burvikovs
Associate Editor:	Desirée Bartlett
Editorial Assistant:	Kimberly Greenberg
Production Editor:	Amy Schroller
Copy Editor:	Teresa Herlinger
Typesetter:	C&M Digitals (P) Ltd.
Proofreader:	Joyce Li
Indexer:	Judy Hunt
Cover Designer:	Michael Dubowe

CONTENTS

PREFACE

ROBERT W. COLE

To me, this eighth volume in *The Soul of Educational Leadership* series, "Leadership for Family and Community Involvement," feels closely related to Volume 6, "Leaders as Communicators and Diplomats." Both volumes feature enormously important roles of education leaders that are often obscured by the everyday demands that clamor for any leader's attention. In Volume 6, a cadre of superintendents and national leaders wrote with firsthand knowledge of the leadership skills necessary to unite disparate followers in common cause. This current volume goes beyond leadership skills to probe the pivotal roles of families and community organizations in school success.

Since our initial discussions early in 2006, the three editors of this series—Paul Houston, Alan Blankstein, and myself—have envisioned this long-term undertaking as providing leaders in education with a toolbox for enriching and sustaining their work. The oft-neglected task of replenishing our personal resources—sharpening our saw, as management guru Tom Peters once said—has been an organizing purpose of this series. From the beginning, we have aimed to provide contributions from leading thinkers and practitioners on the "soul work" of educational leadership.

To that end, Volumes 1 and 2—"Engaging Every Learner" and "Out-of-the-Box Leadership"—emphasized the importance of all students in our society and called for transformative leadership, which can come only by thinking differently about the problems and challenges we face. Subsequent volumes addressed challenging issues that all leaders must confront; "Sustaining Professional Learning Communities" (Volume 3) and "Building Sustainable Leadership Capacity" (Volume 5) acknowledged in their duality the daunting challenge of holding on to and even improving valuable work, and of creating learning communities that have the power to support enduring change. Volumes 4 and 7 covered what might be considered the two extremes in leadership: spirituality and data. Volume 4, "Spirituality in Educational Leadership," acknowledged, as Paul Houston wrote, that "the work we do is really more of a calling and a mission than it is a job." At the opposite end of the leadership spectrum, Volume 7 delved into the nitty-gritty of using data, rather than allowing data to use you.

"Both research and common sense tell us that parents and educators share the same goal—student success—yet strong school/family/community partnerships are often elusive," assert Alan Blankstein and Pedro Noguera in this volume's opening chapter, "Engaging Families to Enhance Student Success." Blankstein, president of the HOPE Foundation (and an editor of this series), and Noguera, the Peter L. Agnew Professor of Education at New York University and an urban sociologist who focuses on the ways in which schools are influenced by urban socioeconomic conditions, call on leaders to transform schools into "welcoming community hubs where every parent feels engaged, every student succeeds, and failure is not an option for any child."

In "Parents as Leaders: School, Family, and Community Partnerships in Two Districts," Mavis Sanders explores parent leadership and the interplay between power and partnerships, identifying factors that have supported the growth and sustainability of parent leadership and engagement. Sanders, assistant professor of education in the School of Professional Studies in Business and Education at Johns Hopkins University and research scientist at the Center for Research on the Education of Students Placed At Risk (CRESPAR), concludes that "Public engagement in education, therefore, is a process that requires preparation and effort from educators as well as district and parent leaders."

Susan Frelick Wooley, Cynthia Rosacker Glimpse, and Sheri DeBoe Johnson, authors of "Sharing the Dream: Engaging Families as

Partners in Supporting Student Success," are, respectively, executive director of the American School Health Association, coordinator of Communities of Practice and Information Services at the Technical Assistance Coordination Center of the Academy for Educational Development, and senior program specialist in family engagement for the National PTA. They caution that decades of research tell us that family involvement is far more than helping with homework, attending parent–teacher conferences, or volunteering in the classroom. They describe "what has and has not worked in partnering between schools and students' families."

"Schools can be more successful, in terms of both academic and social-emotional outcomes, when they help parents foster social-emotional and character development in their children in an emotionally intelligent way," maintain Yoni Schwab and Maurice Elias in "The 'What' and 'How' of Helping Parents Help Students Become Successful Learners." Schwab, a psychologist at the Windward School in White Plains, New York, and at the Institute for Behavior Therapy in New York City, and Elias, a professor of psychology at Rutgers University and vice chair of the Leadership Team of the Collaborative for Academic, Social, and Emotional Learning (CASEL) affirm that "Creativity, knowing the community, and engaging parents in the planning from the beginning are key ingredients to overcoming the obstacles to parent education."

"Both school and public librarians know that neither party can provide all the literacy services that are needed," writes Lesley S. J. Farmer in "Family Literacy: The Roles of School Libraries and Public Libraries." Professor Farmer, who coordinates the Librarianship Program at California State University, Long Beach, and has worked as a teacher-librarian in K–12 school settings as well as in public, special, and academic libraries, adds that "The real issue, therefore, is how to build a successful partnership based on a clear understanding of each librarian's role."

"Planned, regular, two-way communication is essential to building the kind of strong working relationships and active engagement essential to school success and student achievement," asserts Edward Moore in "Balancing Your Communication Ledger: Using Audits to Involve Communities and Build Support for Schools." An associate professor in the College of Communication at Rowan University who has served as associate director of the National School Public Relations Association, Moore advocates that communication audits can ensure "a better understanding of what the community wants both now and in the future."

"Keep small problems small," advises Lin Kuzmich in "Manage the Molehill Before It Becomes a Mountain: Keeping Parent Interactions Productive for Students." An educational consultant, professor, and author from Loveland, Colorado, who also serves as a senior consultant for the International Center for Leadership in Education, Kuzmich notes that "Heading off small problems is about knowing your culture, your staff, your students, and your community." When you do so successfully, you create the opportunity "to be an instructional leader, to form relationships with students and staff, and to become the effective leader you wanted to be in the first place."

In "Raising the Village by Bringing Communities and Schools Together," Paul Houston states the issue very simply: "The key to student success in our fractured world is to find ways to get the community more engaged with children and to get our children more engaged with the community." Houston, recently retired executive director of the American Association of School Administrators, and now president of the Center for Empowered Leadership (and an editor of this series), presents a challenge to leaders: "School leadership today is about understanding that learning is a 24/7 proposition. The school plays an important role as facilitator of learning, but to truly make a difference in the lives of children, the whole 360 degrees of their existence must be taken into consideration."

As we observed in Volume 5, leaders don't lead alone. They must know how to lead others in common cause—and sometimes to remind others throughout any given community what the common cause is toward which we are all working. In this volume, as in the previous volumes in this series, we have amassed examples from decades of research and from exemplary practice to point the way toward success for schools and their communities. The gains to be realized from creating communities and schools that work in partnership are valuable beyond price.

ABOUT THE EDITORS

Paul D. Houston served as executive director of the American Association of School Administrators (AASA) from 1994 to 2008. He is currently president of the Center for Empowered Leadership (CFEL).

Dr. Houston has established himself as one of the leading spokespersons for American education through his extensive speaking engagements, published articles, and regular appearances on national radio and television.

Dr. Houston has coauthored three books: *Exploding the Myths,* with Joe Schneider; *The Board-Savvy Superintendent,* with Doug Eadie; and *The Spiritual Dimension of Leadership,* with Steven Sokolow. He has also authored three books: *Articles of Faith and Hope for Public Education, Outlooks and Perspectives on American Education,* and *No Challenge Left Behind: Transforming America's Schools Through Heart and Soul.*

Dr. Houston was previously a teacher and building administrator in North Carolina and New Jersey. He has also served as assistant superintendent in Birmingham, Alabama, and as superintendent of schools in Princeton, New Jersey; Tucson, Arizona; and Riverside, California.

Dr. Houston has also served in an adjunct capacity for the University of North Carolina, as well as Harvard, Brigham Young, and Princeton Universities. He has been a consultant and speaker throughout the United States and overseas, and he has published more than 200 articles in professional journals.

Alan M. Blankstein is founder and president of the HOPE Foundation, a not-for-profit organization whose honorary chair is Nobel Prize winner Archbishop Desmond Tutu. The HOPE Foundation (Harnessing Optimism and Potential through Education) is dedicated to supporting educational leaders over time in creating school cultures where failure is not an option for any student. HOPE sustains student success.

The HOPE Foundation brought W. Edwards Deming and his work to light in educational circles, beginning with the Shaping Chicago's Future conference in 1988. From 1988 to 1992, in a series of Shaping America's Future forums and PBS video conferences, he brought together scores of national and world leaders including Al Shanker; Peter Senge; Mary Futrell; Linda Darling-Hammond; Ed Zigler; and CEOs of GM, Ford, and other corporations to determine how best to bring quality concepts and those of "learning organizations" to bear in educational systems.

The HOPE Foundation provides professional development for thousands of educational leaders annually throughout North America and other parts of the world, including South Africa. HOPE also provides long-term support for school improvement through leadership academies and intensive on-site school change efforts, leading to dramatic increases in student achievement in diverse settings.

A former "high risk" youth, Blankstein began his career in education as a music teacher and has worked within youth-serving organizations for 20 years, including the March of Dimes, Phi Delta Kappa, and the National Educational Service (NES), which he founded in 1987 and directed for 12 years.

He coauthored with Rick DuFour the *Reaching Today's Youth* curriculum, now provided as a course in 16 states, and has contributed writing to *Educational Leadership, The School Administrator, Executive Educator, High School Magazine, Reaching Today's Youth,* and *EQ + IQ = Best Leadership Practices for Caring and Successful Schools.* Blankstein has provided keynote presentations and workshops for virtually every major educational organization. He is author of the best-selling book *Failure Is Not an Option™: Six Principles That Guide Student Achievement in High-Performing Schools,* which has been named Book of the Year by the National Staff Development Council and was nominated for three other national and international awards.

Blankstein is on the Harvard Principals' Center's advisory board, has served as a board member for the Federation of Families for Children's Mental Health, is a cochair of Indiana University's Neal Marshall Black Culture Center's Community Network, and is advisor to the Faculty and Staff for Student Excellence mentoring program.

He is also an advisory board member for the Forum on Race, Equity, and Human Understanding with the Monroe County Schools in Indiana, and has served on the Board of Trustees for the Jewish Child Care Agency (JCCA) at which he was once a youth-in-residence.

Robert W. Cole is proprietor and founder of Edu-Data, a firm specializing in writing, research, and publication services. He was a member of the staff of *Phi Delta Kappan* magazine for 14 years: assistant editor from 1974–1976, managing editor from 1976–1980, and editor-in-chief from 1981–1988. During his tenure as editor-in-chief, the *Kappan* earned more than 40 Distinguished Achievement Awards from the Association of Educational Publishers, three of them for his editorials.

Since leaving the *Kappan,* Cole has served as founding vice president of the Schlechty Center for Leadership in School Reform (CLSR; 1990–1994). At CLSR, he managed district- and communitywide school reform efforts and led the team that created the Kentucky Superintendents' Leadership Institute. He formed the Bluegrass Leadership Network, in which superintendents worked together to use current leadership concepts to solve reform-oriented management and leadership problems.

As senior consultant to the National Reading Styles Institute (1994–2005), Cole served as editor and lead writer of the Power Reading Program. He and a team of writers and illustrators created a series of hundreds of graded short stories, short novels, and comic books from Primer through Grade 10. Those stories were then recorded by Cole and Dr. Marie Carbo; they are being used by schools all across the United States to teach struggling readers.

Cole has served as a Book Development Editor for the Association for Supervision and Curriculum Development (ASCD), for Corwin, and for Writer's Edge Press. He has been president of the Educational Press Association of America and member of the EdPress Board of Directors. He has presented workshops, master classes, and lectures at universities nationwide, including Harvard, Stanford, Indiana, Xavier, and Boise State Universities, as well as the University of Southern Maine. He has served as a special consultant to college and university deans in working with faculties on writing for professional publication. Recently, he began serving as managing editor and senior associate with the Center for Empowered Leadership.

ABOUT THE CONTRIBUTORS

Maurice J. Elias is a professor of psychology at Rutgers University and vice chair of the Leadership Team of the Collaborative for Academic, Social, and Emotional Learning (CASEL). He is a nationally recognized expert on child and parental problem solving and a writer and contributor to numerous professional publications and magazine and newspaper articles. Elias serves as a trustee of the Association for Children of New Jersey and the HOPE Foundation. He has coauthored the books *Raising Emotionally Intelligent Teenagers: Parenting With Love, Laughter, and Limits* (2000); *Engaging the Resistant Child Through Computers: A Manual for Social and Emotional Learning* (2001); and *Raising Emotionally Intelligent Teenagers: Guiding the Way for Compassionate, Committed, Courageous Adults* (2002). Elias's other involvements include action research on Jewish identity development in children and adolescents and the development and evaluation of video, animation, and computer-based instructional strategies for delivering prevention programs to youth, including those at high risk.

Lesley S. J. Farmer, a professor at California State University, Long Beach, coordinates the Librarianship program. She earned her master's in Library Science at the University of North Carolina at Chapel Hill and received her doctorate in Adult Education from Temple University. Dr. Farmer has worked as a teacher-librarian in K–12 school settings as well as in public, special, and academic libraries. She chaired the Education Section of the Special Libraries Association, and is the International Association of School Librarianship Vice President of Association Relations. A frequent presenter and writer for the profession, Dr. Farmer's research interests include information literacy, collaboration, assessment, and educational technology. Dr. Farmer's most recent book is *Your School Library: Check It Out!* (2009).

Cynthia Rosacker Glimpse is the Coordinator of Social Networking for the Technical Assistance Coordination Center (TACC) at the Academy for Educational Development. Glimpse focuses on communities of practice (CoP) and other social networking strategies. The TACC is funded by the U.S. Department of Education's Office of Special Education Programs.

Glimpse is a member of the American Psychological Association and the IDEA Partnership's CoPs on School-Based Mental Health, Transition, and Creating Agreement, and she is on the Advisory Board of the Center for School Mental Health at the University of Maryland School of Medicine.

She is also a coauthor of the article "Spatio-Temporal Model of Family Engagement: A Qualitative Study of Family-Driven Perspectives on Family Engagement" (*Advances in School Mental Health,* October 2009). Glimpse is a parent of a special education student and worked as a mental health professional prior to focusing on special education.

Sheri DeBoe Johnson has more than 25 years of experience in helping schools identify and implement strategies that integrate health and human services, youth development supports and opportunities, and other expanded learning opportunities that support student success. Throughout her career, she has led or supported the development and implementation of local, state, and national strategies to ensure that children and youth enter school ready to learn every day and transition from school, ready for college or the workforce. Ms. Johnson has managed a variety of strategies to increase awareness and knowledge of what communities can do to help children succeed in school. Examples include recruitment and training of volunteers to monitor educational programs for children in foster care, development of a video to promote a national organization's community school initiative, and conducting workshops and presentations at national conferences on strategies for supporting student success.

In her current position, Ms. Johnson is responsible for conceptualizing and designing tools, resources, and initiatives for a variety of audiences to support student success through effective family and community engagement. Most recently, she led a group of national experts in the field of family and community engagement to develop a rubric based on standards for family engagement. Ms. Johnson continually conducts workshops at local, state, and national conferences and provides updates to national partner networks at various coalition meetings to deepen understanding of and support for family, school, and community partnerships.

Lin Kuzmich is an educational consultant, professor, and author from Loveland, Colorado. She served the Thompson School District in several roles as the assistant superintendent, executive director of secondary and elementary instruction, director of professional development, and a building principal. Her school was named a 2000 winner of the John R. Irwin Award for Academic Excellence and Improvement. In addition, for the past decade she has been involved in staff development through several universities and the Tointon Institute for Educational Change. Kuzmich is an adjunct professor at both Colorado State University and University of Northern Colorado. She is a senior consultant for the International Center for Leadership in Education, has provided training and consulting to school districts around the country, and has presented at numerous national conferences.

Edward H. Moore is an associate professor in the College of Communication at Rowan University. He previously served as associate director of the National School Public Relations Association and managing editor of the newsletter *Communication Briefings*. Moore started his career as a high school journalism teacher and school public relations practitioner. In more than 25 years as an educator, journalist, and public relations counselor, he has written and presented extensively on school public relations issues. Moore is an accredited member of the National School Public Relations Association and the Public Relations Society of America.

Pedro A. Noguera is the Peter L. Agnew Professor of Education at New York University. He holds tenured faculty appointments in the departments of Teaching and Learning and Humanities and Social Sciences at the Steinhardt School of Culture, Education, and Human Development and in the Department of Sociology at New York University. He is also the executive director of the Metropolitan Center for Urban Education and the codirector of the Institute for Globalization and Education in Metropolitan Settings (IGEMS).

He is the author of *The Imperatives of Power: Political Change and the Social Basis of Regime Support in Grenada* (1997); *City*

Schools and the American Dream (2003); *Unfinished Business: Closing the Achievement Gap in Our Nation's Schools* (2006); *City Kids, City Teachers,* with Bill Ayers and Greg Michie (2008); and his most recent book is *The Trouble With Black Boys . . . and Other Reflections on Race, Equity and the Future of Public Education* (2008). Noguera has also appeared as a regular commentator on educational issues on CNN, National Public Radio, and other national news outlets.

Mavis G. Sanders is assistant professor of education in the School of Professional Studies in Business and Education, research scientist at the Center for Research on the Education of Students Placed At Risk (CRESPAR), and senior advisor to the National Network of Partnership Schools at Johns Hopkins University. She is the author of many articles on the effects of school, family, and community support on African American adolescents' school success, the impact of partnership programs on the quality of family and community involvement, and international research on partnerships. She is interested in how schools involve families that are traditionally hard to reach, how schools meet challenges for implementing excellent programs and practices, and how schools define "community" and develop meaningful school–family–community connections. Her most recent book is *Schooling Students Placed at Risk: Research, Policy, and Practice in the Education of Poor and Minority Adolescents* (2000). She earned her PhD in education from Stanford University.

Yoni Schwab is a psychologist at the Windward School in White Plains, New York, and at the Institute for Behavior Therapy in New York City. He earned his doctorate in clinical psychology at Rutgers University and trained at the NYU Child Study Center and at Trinitas Regional Medical Center in New Jersey. His research focuses on the nexus of social-emotional and character development and behavior management, the internalization and generalization of behavior changes, and how social-emotional skills relate to academic achievement. He consults and speaks extensively to school, parent, and community groups on social-emotional and character development, progressive behavior management, and raising the achievement of behaviorally and academically challenged students. He lives in Riverdale, New York, with his wife (a second-grade teacher) and three young, energetic children.

Susan Frelick Wooley, as executive director of the American School Health Association, oversees the day-to-day operations of the national office and represents the association; the school health community; and young people's health concerns as part of coalitions, in contacts with the media, and in advocacy work. She coedited *Health Is Academic: A Guide to Coordinated School Health Programs* (1998), the definitive book on school health, and has authored or coauthored several publications for elementary school–aged children as well as articles for professional publication. She is the immediate past chair of the National Coordinating Committee on School Health and Safety.

Susan Frelick Wooley received her bachelor's degree from Case Western Reserve University, a master's degree from the University of North Carolina at Greensboro, and a PhD in health education from Temple University.

CHAPTER ONE

ENGAGING FAMILIES TO ENHANCE STUDENT SUCCESS

ALAN M. BLANKSTEIN AND PEDRO A. NOGUERA

School leaders today have to be more outward facing than ever before, willing to provide extended school services and work co-operatively with social services, health care professionals, and the local community.

—G. Southworth (2009)

The above quote was part of a "best practices" white paper created by the largest educational leadership organization in the world, based in the United Kingdom. It was written for a group of U.S. leaders who, in February 2009, gathered in Washington to provide the Obama administration with recommendations on the future course of American education.

This perspective, while on target and backed by more research than similar previously published reports, is not entirely new. Consider this quote from the widely publicized 1995 report of the

———————— ❧ ————————

Both research and common sense tell us that parents and educators share the same goal—student success—yet strong school/family/ community partnerships are often elusive. There is no consensus on where the responsibility rests for ensuring parental involvement in schools.

National Education Goals Panel (1995): "By the year 2000, every school will promote partnerships that will increase parental involvement and participation in promoting the social, emotional, and academic growth of children."

Both research and common sense tell us that parents and educators share the same goal—student success—yet strong school/family/ community partnerships are often elusive. There is no consensus on where the responsibility rests for ensuring parental involvement in schools (Blankstein & Noguera, 2010; Harris & Goodall, 2008; Murray, 2009), and the challenges are intellectually simple, but socially complex:

> Low-income parents are often suspicious of schools—they frequently have bad memories of their own time as students—and they commonly have little experience advocating for their children in school. The challenge in low-income communities is often to help parents overcome these suspicions and barriers, whereas the challenge in well-off communities is often to keep overbearing parents from disrupting school functioning. (Weissbourd, 2009b)

But the challenges reside not only with parents. In studying North American and European schools, Andy Hargreaves and Dean Fink tell the story of a powerful and charismatic school principal named Bill Mathews, who was determined to provide "a service to kids and the community." After considerable effort, survey data showed that 95 percent of staff were satisfied with the school, but only 35 percent of students and 25 percent of parents shared that satisfaction (Blankstein, Hargreaves, & Fink, 2010; Hargreaves & Fink, 2003).

Complacency or denial is sometimes a fallback position for an otherwise overburdened or confounded professional staff. How do we cultivate an "outward-facing" perspective among our leaders and teaching staff, and what are the high-leverage activities they can focus on to get the best results?

THREE PRINCIPLES FOR BUILDING POSITIVE SCHOOL–FAMILY RELATIONSHIPS

Schools that take a strategic approach toward becoming community hubs employ three key principles:

1. Mutual understanding based upon empathy and recognition of shared interests

2. Meaningful involvement of family and community in a variety of school activities

3. Regular outreach and communication to family and community

Mutual Understanding and Empathy

The first step toward building or repairing home/school relationships is to gain a common understanding grounded in empathy for students' families. This means that school staff must become aware of the specific challenges that affect many families and make it difficult for them to support their children's learning. Educators must recognize that many parents have had negative experiences with school and are afraid to become involved. They may be intimidated by feelings of ignorance and uncertainty, and they may assume that their children will experience the same kinds of difficulties that they themselves encountered while in school, particularly if their children have special needs (Meehan, Hughes, & Cavell, 2003; Rogers, Wiener, Marton, & Tannock, 2009).

Moreover, many parents are struggling just to make ends meet. Some are working more than one job and have little time to supervise homework. Others are grappling with layoffs, housing foreclosures, and lack of health benefits. Instead of penalizing children and criticizing their parents for lapses and failures in attendance or preparation, the school as community hub works *with* families to extend understanding and support. The understanding invariably comes from creating opportunities for a shared reality: going into the community to engage parents or attending functions of importance to families and their children. Cooperating on a Habitat for Humanity project, artistic production, or sports endeavor together—all are examples that are under way in schools throughout North America. Examples of support may include after-school homework centers, family-friendly schedules and transportation alternatives, comfortable waiting areas with coffee and tea, and translators for school communications and face-to-face meetings.

Meaningful Involvement of Families in the School

According to Barbara Eason-Watkins, making parents feel welcome at school is easier said than done: "In many conversations I've had with parents and members of the community, they felt that most schools didn't want them to participate, didn't want them to be part of the school" (quoted in HOPE Foundation, 2002). Instead of telling parents to drop off their children and return to pick them up at the end of the school day, some schools invite parents in to volunteer. "Shooing parents away tells them, 'we really don't need you here, cut the umbilical cord,'" says school counselor Reggie Rhines at Icenhower Intermediate School in Mansfield, Texas (personal communication, 2009).

This feeling of being unwanted and shut out sometimes stems from parents' own early experiences in school. Those parents who struggled in their own academic careers may feel resentment, distaste, or even anxiety about interacting with school authorities. In other cases, language and cultural differences create barriers that make meaningful parental involvement in schools difficult, if not impossible. Parents who don't speak English may be hesitant to contact schools and unsure of how best to communicate with school personnel about their child's needs. In many cultures, educators are treated as having an authority and status that make families even less willing to ask questions or voice complaints (Blankstein & Noguera, 2010; Elias, Friedlander, & Tobias, 1999; Hill & Tyson, 2009; Noguera, 2003; Valdés, 1996).

Circumstances such as these make it obvious that family involvement in the schools is not something that occurs naturally or easily when cultural, economic, or racial barriers are not addressed. For every parent like educator-physician James Comer's mother, Maggie—whose "American dream" it was to see her children educated despite her minimum-wage salary (Comer, 1989)—there are many more who lack the knowledge, means, and will to make their children's academic success the top priority (Harris & Goodall, 2008; Weissbourd, 2009a).

Meaningful partnerships with parents must be purposely cultivated and planned for, especially when the school's focus is on instructional excellence:

There is a major difference between involving parents in school-ing and engaging parents in learning. While involving parents in school activities has an important social and community func-tion, it is only the engagement of parents in learning in the home that is most likely to result in a positive difference to learning outcomes. (Harris & Goodall, 2008)

Parents can be coached to help students learn to study more effec-tively, including early identification of problem areas, assuring opti-mum environmental factors (such as a consistent, productive study area), and tips on time-management or test-taking strategies. Schools can also cultivate family engagement with academics by bringing parents and other adults in to share their expertise and talents in meaningful ways and by creating parent-to-parent support networks.

Schools that focus on such support networks recognize the value of the contributions that family members can make to the achieve-ment of the school's educational mission. Other strategies for encour-aging meaningful parent involvement include parent-to-parent outreach, parent-led lessons in the diverse languages represented within the school community, parent-led clubs and activities, and par-ent mentoring or tutoring for students who need extra help. Sara Lawrence-Lightfoot (2003) reminds us that this can be as simple as asking parents, "What are *we* going to do to help students?" in place of the more off-putting, "What are *you* going to do?"

Parents or community members can serve as translators to facil-itate communication between the school and non–English-speaking families. Principals and teachers who lack the necessary language skills might also develop partnerships with local churches and com-munity-based organizations to help in doing outreach and providing translation to immigrant parents. Key to this is a genuine belief within the school that it *is* a community hub, as well as a willingness to look outward to the surrounding community to create parental engagement and satisfaction with the school (Department for Children, Schools, and Families [DCSF], 2008; Southworth, 2009).

Inviting parents into the school on a more informal basis can be an opportunity to provide a positive experience, expand the relation-ship between parents and the school, and encourage meaningful and helpful interactions between parents and their children. Reaching out to parents and inviting them into the school, and into the classroom, can inspire a cultural change for teachers. Parents must be given clear guidance on what to do in the classroom so that they do not interfere with teachers, and teacher need to be prepared for the experience as well. Changing the school's culture to embrace and value in-class volunteers is a prerequisite for an effective parent volunteer program. If the teachers don't accept the idea of having parents in the classroom, it simply will not work.

Regular Outreach and Communication to Family and Community

In effective schools, teachers and administrators go the extra mile to reach those children and families whose problems stand in the way of their full involvement in schooling. Part of reaching out is simply making staff members visible in the neighborhood at fast food restaurants, malls, and other places students and families are likely to visit.

Gary Burgess (HOPE Foundation, 2002) says that *wherever* you meet parents—whether at the barbershop, the gym, the church, or the community center—becomes the locus of your campaign to get them into the school. Recruiting parents is not an activity restricted to specific hours at specific places; it is a constant, ongoing process that is central to the operation of the school as a community hub.

Burgess (HOPE Foundation, 2002) recommends a "bring the mountain to Mohammed" approach for providing information about school activities and efforts to the community. In his district, school principals hold periodic informational meetings at local churches and other public meeting places. He notes that these meetings are sometimes better attended than those held at the school because parents and community members perceive them as less threatening and more convenient. Burgess also uses a teacher log to record all parent contacts and then evaluates the information with teachers. By formalizing, valuing, and monitoring these contacts, he has been able to change teachers' behavior.

FIVE EXAMPLES OF WHAT "GOOD" LOOKS LIKE

In spring 2009, the HOPE Foundation conducted a series of telephone conferences with leadership teams located in districts that have comprehensively implemented the "Failure Is Not an Option" principles for at least 2 years. (Failure Is Not an Option is a program that aims to help school leaders create successful, sustainable high-performing schools. The work is designed around six guiding principles: (1) common mission, vision, values, and goals; (2) achievement for all students through prevention and intervention systems; (3) collaborative teaming focused on teaching for learning; (4) data-based decisions for continuous improvement; (5) active family and community engagement; and (6) building sustainable leadership capacity.) Their leadership teams shared various family-engagement strategies they have developed with us.

Monday Morning Newsletter

At Brooks Wester Middle School in Mansfield, Texas, Principal Scott Shafer and teacher leaders transformed their traditional school newsletter into grade-level "e-newsletters" that are distributed every Monday morning via e-mail. The newsletters cover not just school events, but academics, test dates, homework assignments, and contact information for individual teachers.

Designated team members distribute the weekly newsletter and respond to questions from parents who can easily hit "reply" for true interactivity. Students receive extra points on homework assignments for providing e-mail addresses for their parents, and teachers receive a "carrot" as well: "I don't require lesson plans because the newsletters are the lesson plans I need to see," says Shafer. Close to 98 percent of parents now receive the newsletter electronically, with paper copies sent to the 2 percent without online access. On the rare occasions when the newsletter goes out late, the school hears about it from engaged parents. In addition, the school now receives far fewer complaints from parents that they didn't know about student assignments or school events.

Parent Orientations

At the Della Icenhower School (also in Mansfield, Texas), student orientation is called "Ice Camp." But instead of simply telling parents to drop off their children and return to pick them up at the end of the school day, Principal Duane Thurston and the school leadership team now invite family members to attend their own "Ice Camp for Parents." Families get to tour the school and ask any and all questions that come up. "When the kids come home talking about common areas or how and why their lockers are opened, the parents have a better idea. From the beginning of the year we want them to participate," says counselor Reggie Rhines. "We're taking on the Home Depot thing: 'You can do it, we can help'" (personal communication, 2009).

Parent Roundtables

At Williamston Middle School, in the Ingham Independent School District in Michigan, Principal Christine Sermak conducts quarterly roundtable meetings with parents. These meetings take place in the morning or evening, with emphasis on informality. "It's really taken the place of our parent/teacher association," reports Sermak. "I meet with parents, and we talk about things that are going on in the school. It's more parent education and communication, more two-way than me sitting up there with a PowerPoint" (personal communication, 2009).

Movie Night

At Shambaugh Elementary School in Fort Wayne, Indiana, the PTA hosts Movie Nights with a film projector and giant screen in the school gym. This regular event gives staff, students, and parents an opportunity to interact in a very informal setting. "We have amazing attendance," reports Principal Shawn Smiley (personal communication, 2009).

Culture Night

At Icenhower School, each academic team presents its own "Culture Night," celebrating the different continents of the world. The events bring in 60–70 percent of parents because they recognize that their unique cultures and ethnicities are being celebrated. Culture Nights include different foods, artifacts, games, and music. "Parents have really taken a liking to Culture Night," says counselor Reggie Rhines, "because it celebrates who they are and recognizes their culture."

From neighborhood walks that bring educators into the community to car washes that bring community members to the school campus, there are myriad ways for school leaders and teachers to meet families, introduce themselves and their philosophies, and ask parents what they need from the schools to increase engagement. This can serve as a foundation for what ultimately matters most: building family support for student learning.

From neighborhood walks that bring educators into the community to car washes that bring community members to the school campus, there are myriad ways for school leaders and teachers to meet families, introduce themselves and their philosophies, and ask parents what they need from the schools to increase engagement.

GETTING STARTED

As you begin preparing a family and community engagement plan for your school or district, first take a moment to evaluate your current status:

- How many community members participate as members of teams for various improvement activities in your school?
- How many parent volunteers does your school have?
- In what capacities are those volunteers used?
- Of the ethnic and cultural groups forming significant parts of the school population, how many are represented on school teams? As parent volunteers?
- What outreach initiatives have been undertaken to recruit community members, and how effective was each?
- What forums or meetings have been organized to explain school-related issues and answer families' questions?

Consider these strategies for engaging parents in genuine partnerships:

- Change middle and high school handbooks so that they emphasize the positive, identity-building opportunities that await students. Feature interviews and stories with graduates. Place less emphasis on disciplinary infractions, but do present school rules that contribute to the positive identity of the school.

- Develop positive feedback systems to show appreciation of social-emotional intelligence, small amounts of progress, and academic success. Create progress reports about progress of all kinds, and change report cards to include indicators of life skills that parents will understand and appreciate.
- Provide parents with multimedia-formatted guidance with regard to how they can support the work of the school from home.
- Create forums for dialogue about cultural and ethnic differences; create networks of parent liaisons comprising educators, parents, and community residents who can help new families of different ethnic backgrounds adapt to the neighborhood.
- Create opportunities for community service and more meaningful, widely participatory student government. Publicize what happens in these contexts so that parents can see what the school is doing and gain a better understanding of the interests and competencies of their children.
- Provide forums for parent discussions and mutual support around the various developmental issues, familial stressors, and parent–child communication concerns that can be expected during the adolescent years (Elias, Bryan, Patrikakou, & Weissberg, 2003; Elias et al., 1999).

CONCLUSION

We know from experience and research that good teacher–parent relationships improve student learning, development, achievement, and success at school and in later life (Allen, 2007; Blankstein, 2010; Epstein et al., 2008; Sanders, 2006). As educators and leaders, it's up to us to make our schools the welcoming community hubs where every parent feels engaged, every student succeeds, and failure is not an option for any child.

REFERENCES

Allen, J. (2007). *Creating welcoming schools: A practical guide to home–school partnerships with diverse families.* New York: Teachers College Press.

Blankstein, A. M. (2010). *Failure is not an option* (2nd ed.). Thousand Oaks, CA: Corwin.

Blankstein, A. M., Hargreaves, A., & Fink, D. (2010). Building sustainable leadership capacity. In A. M. Blankstein (Ed.), *Failure is not an option* (2nd ed., pp. 189–214). Thousand Oaks, CA: Corwin.

Blankstein, A. M., & Noguera, P. A. (2010). Gaining active engagement from family and community. In A. M. Blankstein (Ed.), *Failure is not an option* (2nd ed., pp. 191–207). Thousand Oaks, CA: Corwin.

Comer, J. P. (1989). *Maggie's American dream: The life of a black family.* New York: Plume.

Department for Children, Schools, and Families (DCSF). (2008). *21st-century schools: World-class education for every child.* London: Author.

Elias, M. J., Bryan, K., Patrikakou, E. N., & Weissberg, R. P. (2003). *Challenges in creating effective home–school partnerships in adolescence: Promising paths for collaboration.* Chicago: Collaborative for Academic, Social, and Emotional Learning.

Elias, M. J., Friedlander, B. S., & Tobias, S. E. (1999). *Emotionally intelligent parenting: How to raise a self-disciplined, responsible, socially skilled child.* New York: Three Rivers Press.

Epstein, J. L., Sanders, M. G., Sheldon, S. B., Simon, B. S., Clark Salinas, K., & Rodriguez Jansorn, N. (2008). *School, family, and community partnerships: Your handbook for action* (3rd ed.). Thousand Oaks, CA: Corwin.

Hargreaves, A., & Fink, D. (2003). Sustaining leadership. *Phi Delta Kappan, 84*(9), 693–700.

Harris, A., & Goodall, J. (2008). Do parents know they matter? Engaging all parents in learning. *Educational Research, 50*(3), 277–289.

Hill, N. E., & Tyson, D. F. (2009). Parental involvement in middle school: A meta-analytic assessment of the strategies that promote achievement. *Developmental Psychology, 45*(3), 740–763.

HOPE Foundation. (2002). *Failure is not an option* [Video series]. Bloomington, IN: Author.

Lawrence-Lightfoot, S. (2003). *The essential conversation: What parents and teachers can learn from each other.* New York: Random House.

Meehan, B. T., Hughes, J. N., & Cavell, T. A. (2003). Teacher–student relationships as compensatory resources for aggressive children. *Child Development, 74,* 1145–1157.

Murray, C. (2009). Parent and teacher relationships as predictors of school engagement and functioning among low-income urban youth. *Journal of Early Adolescence, 29*(3), 376–404.

National Education Goals Panel. (1995). *National Education Goals report: Executive summary.* Washington, DC: Author.

Noguera, P. A. (2003). *City schools and the American dream: Reclaiming the promise of public education.* New York: Teachers College Press.

Rogers, M. A., Wiener, J., Marton, I., & Tannock, R. (2009). Parental involvement in children's learning: Comparing parents of children with and without attention-deficit/hyperactivity disorder (ADHD). *Journal of School Psychology, 47, 167–187.*

Sanders, M. G. (2006). *Building school–community partnerships: Collaboration for student success.* Thousand Oaks, CA: Corwin.

Southworth, G. (2009). *A synthesis of best practices guiding school leadership for 21st-century education: A white paper for the Shaping America's Future forum.* Bloomington, IN: HOPE Foundation.

Valdés, G. (1996). *Con respeto: Bridging the distances between culturally diverse families and schools.* New York: Teachers College Press, 1996.

Weissbourd, R. (2009a). *The parents we mean to be: How well-intentioned adults undermine children's moral and emotional development.* New York: Houghton Mifflin Harcourt.

Weissbourd, R. (2009b, May). The schools we mean to be: Parents and teachers together are powerful vehicles for driving the moral growth of adults and students. *Educational Leadership, 27–31.*

CHAPTER TWO

PARENTS AS LEADERS

*School, Family, and Community Partnerships
in Two Districts*

MAVIS G. SANDERS

D espite significant growth in the research on parent involvement and a general acceptance of its importance in education
reform, parents have been kept at the periphery of education decision
making (for example, see Fine, 1993; Nichols-Solomon, 2000). This
marginalization is largely a result of an unequal distribution of status,
power, and information between parents and professional educators.
While the exclusion of low-income families in education decision
making is most pronounced (see Lareau & Horvat, 1999), families
with greater financial resources are also at risk. More than a decade
ago, Fine observed,

> In current school reform movements, parents do not even enter
> school-based discourse "as if" social equals with educators,
> bureaucrats, or corporate representatives. With some excep-
> tions, the history and contemporary face of public schooling
> suggest their explicit exclusion. Parents feel and are typically
> treated as "less" than the professionals, particularly in low-
> income neighborhoods. In upper-income communities, parents
> are often seen as over-involved and intrusive. (p. 684)

Epstein (quoted in Fine, 1993), however, suggested that status and power differentials can be overcome and parents can become authentic partners in education decision making through a process of partnerships. She argued,

> Distinctions between power and partnership are not mere semantics. The politics of power often yield conflict and disharmony. The politics of partnership stress equity and caring relationships. The two approaches . . . use a different vocabulary for leadership roles and leadership styles, and focus on different outcomes for parents and for children. In building comprehensive programs of partnership we know that those in power must come to care, and those who care must gain some power. (p. 715)

This chapter explores parent leadership and the interplay between power and partnerships in an urban district in the Northeast and a suburban district in the Midwest. It reviews definitions of leadership and power, and then draws on qualitative case study data to describe how parent leadership has influenced school, family, and community partnerships.[1] The concluding section of this chapter identifies factors that have supported the growth and sustainability of parent leadership and engagement in the two districts. Both districts have been members of the National Network of Partnership Schools (NNPS) for more than a decade.

THE NATIONAL NETWORK OF PARTNERSHIP SCHOOLS

NNPS was established in 1996 to build the capacity of school, district, and state education leaders to develop comprehensive and

[1]Research reported in this chapter was supported by a grant from the U.S. Department of Education, Institute of Education Sciences. The opinions expressed are the author's and do not necessarily represent the positions or policies of the funding agency. The author would like to sincerely thank participants for their willing cooperation at each stage of the study. Actual names of districts and individuals involved in the study are not used so as to ensure participant anonymity and confidentiality.

permanent school, family, and community partnership programs. Such programs require that professional educators acknowledge and support the important role of families and communities in the learning process. Accordingly, the NNPS approach to partnerships requires a fundamental shift in how schools work by extending traditional collegial and teacher/student talk to teacher/student/parent/community talk about matters related to teaching and learning.

The NNPS approach comprises three core principles. The first of these is a broad definition of parent and community involvement based on Epstein's (1995) framework of six types of involvement: (1) parenting, (2) communicating, (3) volunteering, (4) learning at home, (5) decision making, and (6) collaborating with the community. The second core NNPS principle is a team approach (including principals, teachers, and family representatives) to partnership program development and design (Sanders & Epstein, 2000). The third principle is a research-driven approach to school, family, and community partnerships to achieve important goals for students (see Epstein et al., 2009).

When districts and states join NNPS, they are responsible for coordinating partnership programs at their respective levels. District facilitators also are guided to provide ongoing professional development to school-based partnership teams. These teams are responsible for planning, implementing, evaluating, and sustaining school-level partnership programs that incorporate NNPS's three core principles. (For more information, visit www.partnershipschools.org/.)

LEADERSHIP AND SCHOOL, FAMILY, AND COMMUNITY PARTNERSHIPS

Broadly defined, leadership is the exercise of influence to help an organization or group achieve its objectives. In the field of education, leadership is valued when it is directed toward helping schools reach important goals for students' learning and development. Progressive members of society are further interested in leadership focused on equitable educational opportunities and outcomes for students regardless of race, socioeconomic status, sexual orientation, disability, or other traits associated with discrimination in the larger society.

Collaborative leadership, or the sharing of leadership responsibilities among multiple stakeholders . . . is a vehicle for achieving excellent and equitable schooling.

Collaborative leadership, or the sharing of leadership responsibilities among multiple stakeholders (see Gray, 1991; Rubin, 2002), is a vehicle for achieving excellent and equitable schooling. It is a critical component of comprehensive programs of school, family, and community partnerships, which require administrators, teacher leaders, parent leaders, and others to work together to identify and achieve important goals for children and adolescents.

Yet many educators remain resistant to parent leadership and participation. They view it as an unwelcome intrusion on their professional space rather than an opportunity for collaborative action on the behalf of students. Comer (2005) observed,

> Some schools want parents to cooperate by keeping their children under control but resist involving the parents in discussions about school organization, management, culture, teaching, and learning. When parents receive these mixed or disingenuous messages, they sense that they are unwanted. Thus, many schools that believe they are encouraging parents to participate nevertheless find that the parents don't respond. (p. 39)

Thus, schools and districts often create self-fulfilling prophecies regarding parent leadership and participation. Due to the absence of trust and an operating framework of partnerships with which to forge constructive collaboration, public schools often find themselves bereft of an engaged and supportive "public." Instead, many of these schools face disengaged, resentful, or angry parents; diminishing resources; unsympathetic policies; and students who fail to meet the learning standards required for success in the 21st century. While developing trust and implementing a framework of partnerships is entirely possible, it requires the sharing of resources, information, and (equally important) power.

POWER AND SCHOOL, FAMILY, AND COMMUNITY PARTNERSHIPS

Fine (1993) criticized the conspicuous absence of discussions of power in the literature on school, family, and community partnerships.

In a review of three parental involvement initiatives, she found that issues of power, authority, and control limited the impact of these initiatives to improve educational practices and outcomes for broad populations of students. She concluded,

> The presumption of equality between parents and schools and the refusal to address power struggles has systematically undermined real educational transformation, and has set up parents as well as educators involved with reform. In scenes in which power asymmetries are not addressed and hierarchical bureaucracies are not radically transformed, parents end up looking individually "needy," "naïve," or "hysterical" and appear to be working in opposition to teachers. . . . Rarely do they have the opportunity to work collaboratively with educators inventing what could be a rich, engaging, and democratic system for education. (p. 684)

Noguera (2004) observed that, within urban contexts, greater power is possessed by school authorities than by students' parents and communities due to the unequal distribution of material and nonmaterial resources in the form of financial, political, and social capital; time; and information. Other examinations of the topic suggest that parents' power originates and manifests itself differently from the power that resides with school practitioners. Lake and Billingsley (2000) argued that in public schools, parents' power often stems from legislation such as the Individuals with Disabilities Education Act (IDEA), whereas the power of schools and districts stems from their positions, control of information, and access to school resources and personnel. Each stakeholder, then, has *some* power regarding the education of children. The degree of power possessed by any individual differs according to his or her professional position, social and human capital, and sense of efficacy.

How power is used has a great deal to do with the effectiveness of partnership programs. For school, family, and community partnership programs to be successful, all individuals must understand their power, the source(s) of their power, differences in power, and the most constructive ways to use their power to move partnerships forward and advance the quality of education for all children. In this regard, Warren (2005) advocates for the use of relational power. *Relational power* is the power to achieve goals through collective action, in contrast to unilateral power or achieving goals by exerting dominance over others. Relational power comes from understanding the organizations or people with whom one seeks to work and acting as an equal partner in creating shared visions and addressing critical issues. When education, community, and parent leaders exercise relational power, they help forge the types of interpersonal relationships and networks necessary for effective school, family, and community partnerships. The following sections of this chapter describe how the use of relational power by school, district, and parent leaders has influenced the quality of school, family, and community partnerships in the two districts being discussed.

PARTNERSHIP PROGRAM DEVELOPMENT

The Urban District

The urban school district, located in the northeastern United States, is a former industrial area that declined in economic prosperity and population during the last half of the 20th century. According to 2000 U.S. census data, approximately 293,000 people, and 67,000 families reside in the city. The racial makeup is about 54 percent European American, 37 percent African American, 1 percent Asian American, 8 percent from other races or from two or more races, and 8 percent Latino of any race. The urban district includes 60 schools that serve approximately 38,000 students.

The district joined NNPS in 1999 as part of its systemwide improvement efforts. One of the district's family involvement coordinators explained,

> When . . . [the district] was going through their initial school improvement process, school teams trained with a specialist in school improvement. . . . There was one piece that was missing from the training—nowhere did it have a place for parents. How were parents and families going to help the school achieve their goals? We knew that if we were really going to make a difference we had to have the parents on board with us. So there was some research as to strategy we could use for parent involvement and we settled on NNPS. (Personal communication, Fall 2005)

Under the leadership of its superintendent, widely described as an "advocate for family engagement," the district joined NNPS with a majority of its elementary schools and three district family involvement coordinators participating. The coordinators received training to implement the NNPS partnership approach from the organization's director and facilitators.

The family involvement coordinators conducted several activities as NNPS district members, including quarterly cluster meetings to provide support and guidance to school-based partnership teams, end-of-year celebration meetings to provide school partnership teams the time and opportunity to reflect on progress and plan future initiatives, and workshops to build the capacity of families and educators for partnerships. The quality of such activities and the number of school members participating in the district's chapter of NNPS increased each year. In recognition of these accomplishments, the district received an award for excellence from NNPS.

"How were parents and families going to help the school achieve their goals? We knew that if we were really going to make a difference we had to have the parents on board with us."

The district's work on partnerships and its ability to sustain the reform for more than a decade has been partly the result of its relationship with a community-based parent involvement organization (CPIO), whose cochairs received NNPS training along with the district's family involvement coordinators. The CPIO is an ethnically diverse organization supported primarily by Title I funds allocated to the district. As required in its bylaws, the organization is made up of parent leaders from each school in the district. The CPIO conducted a variety of activities that provided members with information on state standards, family and community involvement, school leadership, and education terminology. These activities included a book club, professional development retreat, and monthly meetings where parent leaders shared "promising" partnership practices. The meetings also served as venues where the district's family involvement coordinator(s) and the superintendent or a designee were available to discuss important issues and concerns in the district (see Sanders, 2009a).

The Suburban District

The suburban school district, located in the Midwest, comprises about 21 schools serving approximately 19,000 students. According to 2000 U.S. census data, the district has a population of about

130,000 residents, the median family income is $89,000, and the median home value is $254,000. Among individuals 25 and older, about 96 percent have received a high school diploma or higher and about 61 percent have received a bachelor's degree or higher. Less than half of 1 percent live below the poverty level. The population is predominantly European American (85.2 percent), with a growing Asian population (9.6 percent) and smaller African American (3 percent) and Hispanic (3 percent) populations.

It would be easy to conclude that school, family, and community partnerships occurred "naturally" in this affluent suburban school district. This conclusion would be incorrect, however, which is what school officials learned in 1994 when a referendum to increase the Education Fund tax rate failed. The referendum asked voters for a 35-cent increase to finance a technology plan, pay off a deficit in the Education Fund, reduce class size, and create a reserve fund. The referendum was defeated resoundingly: 17,943 to 8,233.

Through a series of focus groups, district education leaders found that families and communities felt isolated from the schools and that better communication and more meaningful collaboration were needed. The district then joined NNPS and has been a member since 1996. Since joining NNPS, the district has won the NNPS award for excellence numerous times. Selection has been based on the quality of district-level activities implemented by the district's Core Leadership Team (CLT).

The CLT is cochaired by a parent and a school principal. According to the current director of community relations, who serves as the district liaison to NNPS, the cochair approach, in which parents and principals equally share leadership responsibilities, helps to prevent the development of an "us against them" environment within the school system. Parents—representing elementary, middle, and high schools—compose one-third of the CLT members and play a vital role on the leadership team. They represent the team at national and local meetings and help to plan and coordinate professional development, funding, and other forms of support provided to school-based partnership teams. Parents also act as leaders on school-based partnership teams, receiving training alongside building administrators in order to carry out their responsibilities as partners in school-level decision making (see Sanders, 2009b).

Parent Leadership and School, Family, and Community Partnerships

The Urban District

Parent leadership in the urban school district has helped to sustain the district's partnership efforts through budget crises, as well as major changes in staffing and leadership. Through their actions on school-based partnership teams and in the CPIO, parent leaders have worked collaboratively to ensure that, despite these difficulties, schools have remained focused on working with families and communities to support students' learning. For example, parent leaders in the CPIO pushed through an initiative to ensure that every school in the district had a planned function to welcome families at the beginning of the school year. According to a family involvement coordinator,

> [The CPIO] has been very, very supportive in building school, family, and community partnerships in the district. . . . For example, we started a big campaign three years ago about starting the school year off right and welcoming parents with first-week activities. . . . It took us about three years before we really got schools to turn in plans before the first day of school outlining what they were going to do to make parents and families feel welcome in their buildings that first week. But we worked at it. We kept at it. It started small with just a few schools. But the [CPIO] was relentless about it; they wanted it. We kept working at it until it finally got to the point where it became mandatory that every building needed to do something. (Personal communication, Fall 2005)

CPIO parent leaders also strengthened communication at their schools by sharing important information with the larger school community. The following exchange with a CPIO member illustrates how such sharing occurred:

Barbara: I find that with each [CPIO] meeting I go to, there is always something new, some new insight, something that people should be aware of, and I am hoping that as members we can turn around and communicate it to other parents who can't be there. . . .

Interviewer: Have you found yourself sharing the information?

Barbara: Yes, like this meeting [a Board of Education meeting focused on the school budget], I wanted my son's school to know about it, so I made a flyer and asked, "Will you pass them out to parents?" And they said, "Oh sure," and they did it. They copied it and got it out to the parents and that was fantastic. That is a great example of the best way that the parents and schools can work together to get information out and help the parents be involved. (Personal communication, Fall 2006)

CPIO members also assisted their school partnership teams in implementing practices that focused on students' learning. One parent coordinator described the impact of CPIO members on school partnership teams in the following way:

I have found that parents who attend CPIO meetings are joining partnership teams in their buildings, which has been strongly encouraged. . . . [The CPIO] also has really embraced the best-practice concept, and that sharing best practice is good. At the [CPIO] meetings, they talk very knowledgeably about best practices and activities that they either initiated or were very supportive of that were helping the schools reach their school improvement goals—their goals for reading and math. (Personal communication, Fall 2005)

The impact of parent leadership has also been felt at the district level. CPIO parent leaders helped to ensure that the superintendent did not allow school, family, and community partnerships to be pushed to the periphery of his reform agenda. They met with him monthly and actively advocated for the district to fill family involvement coordinator positions that were vacant due to two retirements in the course of 2 years. The CPIO parent leaders worked with the family involvement coordinator, Title I director, and other parent and community leaders to develop a road map for parent involvement in the district. The committee

Parent leaders helped to ensure that the superintendent did not allow school, family, and community partnerships to be pushed to the periphery of his reform agenda.

produced a report recommending areas for improvement, including establishing an office of parent involvement, hiring a director for that office, and funding a parent liaison position for each school (including high schools that had not been formally involved in the district's partnership efforts) in the district.

Parent leaders in the district labored so hard on these issues because of their passion for education and the larger community. This passion was expressed by one parent leader, who explained,

> Honestly, I've always enjoyed education. I always enjoyed the thought that you could really be successful if you just did well in school. I mean, if you really keep going, you would be successful. I don't know—growing up . . . [here], I just love the community. I loved the potential I saw around me. I look at myself and truly equate it with . . . [the city]. I mean, I started and my circumstances weren't perfect, but through the educational process, I was able to learn more and broaden my horizons and find out that, you know, things are do-able. They may not be do-able the way that you think, you have to think outside of the box, but they can be done so I wanted to come and bring that back. (Personal communication, Spring 2007)

The Suburban District

In the suburban school district, the impact of parent leadership was evident in 2002 when parent leaders organized hundreds of parents, teachers, administrators, senior citizens, students, and community members in a collaborative effort to ensure that the next education tax-rate referendum passed. The 2002 referendum ultimately passed with a margin of over 2,000 votes in an election that drew the biggest voter turnout of any non-primary election in the district's history.

However, the benefits of parent leadership have been visible not only at the polls, but at the district central office and in the schools as well. The CLT sponsored or cosponsored a variety of activities to assist parent leaders, teachers, and administrators in working collaboratively to support students' learning. These activities included professional development workshops on cultural diversity and competence, working with the media, and data-based decision making. These activities were held regularly and are perceived as having a positive effect on the quality of family engagement and school partnership activities.

The district's director of community relations emphasized the important role of professional development for parent leadership in the district. She explained,

> The parents love being at the data retreats and the professional development workshops. They love being at the table, and as a result they have a higher level of appreciation for the teachers and the principal. That is what I have heard from the parents—that they never really knew what teachers did. They just saw the classroom. Before the action teams, many parents didn't know what a school improvement plan was; now they do. . . . Now we are getting parents engaged in the business of education. It was difficult for schools to open up and share their dirty laundry and to have the trust to say to families, "This is a hole that we have and we need your help to fill it." And now when the Curriculum Office plans professional development workshops, they structure the day to accommodate parents' schedules and meaningful family involvement. (Personal communication, Fall 2007)

School-based partnership activities in the district ranged from academic support and enrichment for students' learning in the elementary and middle grades to student internships and job-shadowing opportunities in the high schools (see Sanders, 2009b). Because parents cochaired the school-based partnership teams, their input into these activities and decision making at the school level was critical. When discussing their importance, a high school partnership team cochair stated, "The action teams at this school are exemplary. I cannot tell you enough about the quality of work that they are doing and how impactful it is for our school and our students" (personal communication, Winter 2009).

An elementary school principal credited the school's action team, which she cochaired with two parents, with helping the school meet important goals for students. She stated,

> The team takes the angst away from how to implement the school improvement plans. . . . I used to have stomach issues over the school improvement plan in my former school, but now

I don't. I can't do it all alone—but look what 40 parents can do. We get so much accomplished and have fun doing it. (Personal communication, Spring 2008)

The parents and teachers on the action team served 2-year terms in a process that helped the school to maintain key partnership activities while adding new ones to address the changing needs of local families. Parent leaders also interacted with the district coordinator and superintendent to share information and ideas.

The parent cochairs of the action team explained these school and district responsibilities in an interview conducted in spring 2008:

Parent 1: We ask families, what are the programs that you want? What has worked for you? We take that data and include it in our planning every spring for how we address goals in the school improvement plan. . . . We meet 5 times a year but most of the work is done by committees on the team who work outside of these meetings. . . .

Parent 2: We keep all our data and activity descriptions in the binder the district gave us so that we can pass it on to the next set of leaders. . . . We usually attend district meetings 3 or 4 times a year for parent leaders, and we also serve on the superintendent's parent advisory board. The board includes all action-team parent co-chairs and home-and-school presidents and meets about 3 to 4 times a year. . . . It's like being a part of the family. It is fun and a nice way to touch base and get together with other parents in the district.

The CLT helped to sustain parent leadership in the district through its rotating leadership structure. Cochairs-elect served on the CLT and observed the acting cochairs for a year before taking office. They then held the position for a year before being replaced by the next team of elected leaders. Once their tenure on the CLT ended, parent leaders regularly took leadership positions on their school-based teams at the elementary, middle, and high school levels. When describing the significance of this leadership structure, one parent leader on a junior high school partnership team commented, "Being on the CLT really helped me. . . . It is invaluable the support members offer. . . . It is a really nice relationship between the district and school" (personal communication, Spring 2008).

DISTRICT FACTORS INFLUENCING
PARENT LEADERSHIP AND ENGAGEMENT

*Active support from the
superintendent and school board
has been a key feature of the
districts' partnership programs,
and clearly related to their success
in creating a collaborative culture
in which family members and
professional educators work as
partners in the educational
process.*

Data suggest that both districts have been able to maintain high levels of parent leadership and engagement by emphasizing a partnership model and ethos consistent with the NNPS approach. Analyses highlight several factors that may explain the districts' success in doing so. These are (1) active support by the superintendent and school board, (2) coordinator leadership and advocacy, (3) NNPS support, and (4) time.

1. Active Support by the Superintendent and School Board

"I don't care what anyone says, you are not going to get anywhere if you don't have the school board and superintendent with you. . . . We were lucky to have a superintendent and school board who let parents know that they were needed and appreciated" (former director of community relations, Suburban School District; personal communication, January 2007). As this quote suggests, active support from the superintendent and school board in both districts has been a key feature of the districts' partnership programs, and clearly related to their success in creating a collaborative culture in which family members and professional educators work as partners in the educational process. This top-level support and engagement in partnership activities have resulted in a climate of accountability and high expectations for partnerships, as well as funding for the infrastructure necessary to build and sustain partnerships over time.

A former officer and current member of the CPIO commented that support from the district partnership coordinators and the superintendent was the CPIO's "greatest strength." The former director of the CPIO elaborated,

[T]he superintendent . . . understands the necessity of parent involvement much the same as [the former superintendent], so we didn't miss a beat. As a matter of fact, he has been a lot more active in the "Superintendent Update" section of our meetings because the former superintendent had to travel a great deal. To date, this superintendent has done every update himself. (Personal communication, Spring 2006)

2. Coordinator Leadership and Advocacy

While top-level support is certainly necessary and beneficial, without the commitment of district family involvement coordinators, whose primary responsibilities include development of districtwide partnership programs, the level and quality of partnerships and parental engagement could not be developed or sustained. Both districts have benefited from the work of exemplary family involvement coordinators, who are responsible for partnership program development. Because of their deep knowledge of the field, diverse leadership experiences, and commitment to the principles and goals of partnerships, these individuals have been able to build stakeholders' understanding of and capacity for collaboration at the district and school levels.

Through the coordination of training and professional development opportunities; the modeling of collaborative behavior; and the building of personal relationships and diverse networks of parents, business leaders, and professional educators, the family involvement coordinators have been the "glue" that has held the districts' partnership programs together. A junior high school principal in the suburban district described the importance of the coordinator's position in the following statement:

> The district has actually put its money where its mouth is because they hired [name of reform leader] to be a central office administrator. How many districts do that? I don't know many. So I think that one huge blessing that we have is that because of our size, we are able to have support. If I need help with something I can always call [name of reform leader], and she will always help you. (Personal communication, Spring 2009)

3. NNPS Support

NNPS has clearly influenced the development of partnerships in the two districts. Parent, school, and district leaders have consistently attended the organization's leadership and training conferences.

NNPS in turn has provided tools, information, and professional development opportunities that helped to minimize the knowledge gap between educators and family and community leaders. By reducing this gap, power differentials that can create barriers to partnerships have been reduced.

Family involvement coordinators worked closely with NNPS staff to organize and deliver partnership team trainings and professional development workshops in the two districts. This close relationship has helped the districts to disseminate widely a message of collaboration and partnership. It has also helped the districts to gain the support of some resistant administrators. As the former family involvement coordinator in the suburban district noted, "Egos can get in the way, but clear, concise thinking on the part of NNPS helped many principals understand parent involvement" (personal communication, Winter 2007). Thus, through training parents and educators side by side, and providing a research-based structure for partnerships, NNPS helped the districts move toward more authentic partnerships between parent and school leaders.

4. Time

Time—in terms of the time designated for professional development on, and implementation and evaluation of, partnerships as well as the passage of time—helped the districts in their partnership efforts. Time has given key stakeholders the opportunity to build common vocabulary, skills, and knowledge to promote parent engagement and leadership throughout the districts. Time has also given more school principals the needed space to adjust to what was, for many, a different and alien leadership approach and style. Traditionally, principal leadership has been characterized by control: Effective leaders were perceived as those who could successfully control teachers, students, and parents. With time, many principals in the districts reportedly adapted to the collaborative leadership style required for authentic school, family, and community partnerships. This adaptation was supported in the suburban district when principal leadership for school, family, and community partnerships was added to the annual principal evaluation. While school, family, and community partnerships were not a part of principal evaluation in the urban district, time has resulted in the retirement of the more recalcitrant principals.

Time was also needed for principals to trust that parents were focused on home–school partnerships for students' success, not parental control of school functions. As one leader observed, "What I found was that often the parents trusted the principal, but the principal did not trust the parents." One high school parent leader in the suburban district believed that building trust was a two-way street; she described her efforts to be trustworthy in the following way:

Parent Leader: I think that as a parent coming in, I need to develop trust with the school leadership. What I mean by that is they need to know by my behavior that I am not going to waste their time. So it's been very important to me that every single time I meet with school leadership, I am prepared and have objectives set, and we pay attention to time. I personally believe that that is how . . . Rob and Tom [the principal and assistant principal] after a while knew that I wouldn't waste their time. So having experienced this, I cannot overemphasize how important that is. It is about preparation. (Personal communication, Spring 2009)

Over time, principals in both districts have responded to superintendent and school board expectations for partnerships, benefited from the work of the district partnership coordinators and NNPS training, and experienced the positive results and additional resources made available through partnerships. In the process, many have become comfortable with and advocates for parental engagement and leadership. As a junior high school principal in the suburban district explained, "Why wouldn't a principal want parent leadership? I don't know everything. When we need to accomplish something, it's great to have great people—parents, faculty, and administrators—who can get it done!" (personal communication, Spring 2009).

> *Over time, principals in both districts have responded to superintendent and school board expectations for partnerships, benefited from the work of the district partnership coordinators and NNPS training, and experienced the positive results and additional resources made available through partnerships.*

CONCLUSION

These two districts illustrate how cultures of partnership—in which principals, district leaders, and parent leaders use relational power—can develop over time. Parent leaders in these districts are not observers, pushed to the margins of schooling. They are active participants in helping schools to identify important goals for students and their families and to achieve those goals through purposeful action.

District, school, and parent leaders had to work over a period of time for the success they experienced. District leaders and school leaders have had to open their doors to public engagement. This has meant that they have created opportunities and structures that support family involvement. Family leaders have also had to work to ensure that they are prepared to help schools move forward in meaningful ways for students.

Public engagement in education, therefore, is a process that requires preparation and effort from educators as well as district and parent leaders. Principals and teachers require professional development on school, family, and community partnerships to ensure that they are prepared to work collaboratively to support the kind of parent leadership and participation that research and practice show results in benefits for students. District leaders need professional and networking opportunities to learn more about how to promote collaborative decision making and problem solving at a systemic level. Parents also need information, support, and opportunities to be effective leaders within increasingly bureaucratic and data-driven systems. Only through such broad-based effort can public engagement achieve its promise for education progress and transformation.

REFERENCES

Comer, J. (2005, March). The rewards of parent participation. *Educational Leadership,* 38–42.

Epstein, J. L. (1995, May). School/family/community partnerships: Caring for the children we share. *Phi Delta Kappan, 76*(9), 701–712.

Epstein, J. L., Sanders, M. G., Sheldon, S. B., Simon, B. S., Salinas, K. C., Jansorn, N. R., et al. (2009). *School, family, and community partnerships: Your handbook for action* (3rd ed.). Thousand Oaks, CA: Corwin.

Fine, M. (1993). [Ap]parent involvement: Reflections on parents, power, and urban public schools & responses. *Teachers College Record, 94*(4), 682–729.

Gray, B. (1991). *Collaborating: Finding common ground for multiparty problems.* San Francisco: Jossey-Bass.

Lake, J., & Billingsley, B. (2000). An analysis of factors that contribute to parent–school conflict in special education. *Remedial and Special Education, 21*(4), 240–251.

Lareau, A., & Horvat, E. (1999). Moments of social inclusion and exclusion: Race, class, and cultural capital in family–school relationships. *Sociology of Education, 72*(1), 37–53.

Nichols-Solomon, R. (2000). Conquering the fear of flying. *Phi Delta Kappan, 82*(1), 19–21.

Noguera, P. (2004, October 17). Transforming urban schools through investments in the social capital of parents. *In Motion Magazine.* Retrieved February 28, 2010, from http://inmotionmagazine.com/er/pn_parents.html.

Rubin, H. (2002). *Collaborative leadership.* Thousand Oaks, CA: Corwin.

Sanders, M. G. (2009a). Collaborating for change: How an urban school district and a community-based organization support and sustain school, family, and community partnerships. *Teachers College Record, 111*(7), 1693–1712.

Sanders, M. G. (2009b). District leadership and school–community collaboration. In A. Honigsfeld & A. Cohan (Eds.), *Breaking the mold of school instruction and organization: Innovative and successful practices for the 21st century* (pp. 139–147). Lanham, MD: Rowman & Littlefield.

Sanders, M. G., & Epstein, J. L. (2000). National Network of Partnership Schools: How research influences educational practice. *Journal of Education for Students Placed at Risk, 5*(1 & 2), 61–76.

Warren, M. (2005). Communities and schools: A new view of urban education reform. *Harvard Educational Review, 75*(2), 133–175.

CHAPTER THREE

SHARING THE DREAM

*Engaging Families as Partners in
Supporting Student Success*

SUSAN FRELICK WOOLEY,
CYNTHIA ROSACKER GLIMPSE,
AND SHERI DEBOE JOHNSON

Becoming concerned about the increased incidence of obesity among the students, Principal Stevens of Middletown School decided that a campaign to educate students' families, especially mothers, was in order. The campaign, planned and conducted in collaboration with a local dietician, included an article in the parent newsletter that provided ideas for nutritious snacks and suggestions for bag lunches, an after-school cooking demonstration with the chef of a local restaurant using affordable and easy-to-prepare ingredients, homework assignments for students to engage their parents in determining the nutrient content of a day's food, and e-mail reminders sent via the school's parent alert system.

While ambitious and well-intentioned, the above scenario ignored several key factors when it came to family engagement. The first problem was the assumption of family deficiency and school superiority. The principal's actions followed the deficit-based model that is prevalent in so many schools' interactions with the public, as opposed to dealing with families in a way that recognizes their strengths. The actions above implied that families lack knowledge of how to provide appropriate food choices for their children and that the school "knew best."

A second problem was that no one in the target population was involved in planning and implementing the campaign. As advocates of disability rights say, "Not about me without me." Involvement of all stakeholders leads to greater investment and stronger collaborative relationship among everyone involved. A dietician certainly was a valuable ally and ensured that accurate information was shared. However, what parents might want or need was never taken into account. Furthermore, the afternoon cooking demonstration would not fit the schedules of many working parents. The emphasis on affordable and easy-to-prepare ingredients was commendable, but cultural and ethnic dietary preferences and practices were not considered.

Another assumption made by the principal was that the increase in obesity was due solely to diet; no changes in physical activity were suggested, even though the connection between physical inactivity and obesity is undisputed. Increasing levels of physical activity is a shared responsibility among schools, families, and communities. Schools can contribute by providing physical education, scheduling recess, incorporating physical activity into various lesson plans, and making facilities available to families and community groups after school hours. Families in which the adults are physically active tend to have children who are more physically active. Families can encourage and support their children's participation in activities that involve physical activity and can limit time spent watching television and sitting in front of computers. Families, in other words, might have desired some collaboration around increasing opportunities for physical activity.

Family involvement is often thought of simplistically as helping with homework, attending parent–teacher conferences, or volunteering in the classroom. More than 30 years of research tells us that it is so much more than that.

Family involvement is often thought of simplistically as helping with homework, attending parent–teacher conferences, or volunteering in the classroom. More than 30 years of research tells us that it is so much more than that. Just as teachers and school administrators provide leadership in the classroom, in the school, and at the school district level—with the goal of academic success for every student—parents also must be engaged, equal partners in order to achieve this goal. While all parents might not feel comfortable taking on a leadership role on their own, organized parent leadership has the ability to mobilize greater involvement and investment from parents and community and affect policies and practices that support and sustain academic success.

This chapter examines the research on effective ways of engaging families in their children's education and what has and has not worked in partnering between schools and students' families. It includes descriptions of common patterns of interactions and barriers to partnership, and suggests some concrete actions that school and family leaders can take.

EFFECTIVE WAYS TO CONNECT SCHOOLS, FAMILIES, AND COMMUNITIES

In a synthesis of research on family engagement, key findings by Henderson and Mapp (2002) on effective strategies for connecting schools, families, and communities included the following:

- "Programs that successfully connect with families and communities invite involvement, are welcoming, and address specific parent and community needs" (p. 43).
- "Parent involvement programs that are effective in engaging diverse families recognize, respect, and address cultural and class differences" (p. 48).
- "Effective programs to engage families and communities embrace a philosophy of partnership. The responsibility for children's educational development is a collaborative enterprise among parents, school staff, and community members" (p. 51).
- "Organized initiatives to build parent and community leadership to improve low-performing schools are developing in low-income urban areas and the rural South. These community organizing efforts use strategies that are aimed at establishing a power base to hold schools and school districts accountable for low student achievement. They have contributed to changes in policy, resources, personnel, school culture, and educational programs" (p. 53).

Schools that succeed in engaging all types of families from diverse backgrounds share key practices identified by Henderson and Mapp (2002). They

- "focus on building trusting collaborative relationships among teachers, families, and community members";
- "recognize, respect, and address families' needs, as well as class and cultural difference"; and
- "embrace a philosophy of partnership where power and responsibility are shared" (p. 7).

In *Beyond the Bake Sale: The Essential Guide to Family–School Partnerships* (Henderson, Mapp, Johnson, & Davies, 2006), the authors identified four approaches that schools tend to take in engaging students' families:

- *Fortress schools* (which see parents as the cause of their children's failure and as uncooperative);
- *Come-if-we-call schools* (which invite parents to open houses and in which staff members provide parent education);
- *Open-door schools* (where teachers hold twice-yearly conferences with parents, and parents raise issues at PTA meeting or meetings with school administrators); and
- *Partnership schools* (where teachers visit students in their homes, a clear process exists for resolving problems, and parents and teachers research issues together). When parents are full partners in their children's education at home and at school, their children are more likely to perform better academically and on tests, take higher-level courses, and graduate from high school and go on to postsecondary education.

BARRIERS TO EFFECTIVE PARTNERSHIPS

Many barriers can end up becoming roadblocks to engagement. When the experience of families is not valued, that can lead to limited and negative communication. When the system seeks only to involve families in a surface way that does not lead to ongoing communication and collaboration, then the power that comes from everyone working together is diluted. When only the easy-to-engage family members are reached, the children of marginalized adults often fail to connect with schools.

Too many teachers and school administrators actually *fear* interactions with students' families, and sometimes view family members as adversaries rather than as partners. School leaders who are serious about family engagement need to be clear about their own philosophical and cultural grounding in this respect.

Building true partnerships and sharing power for decision making requires trust. In communities where many adults had negative experiences with schools and schooling, educators must work even harder to develop that trust. Such adults include those who did not attend school (e.g., some immigrants from developing countries), struggled in school (e.g., school dropouts or push-outs), were not connected to school (e.g., the loner or the victim of bullying who was not supported by school staff), or

Building true partnerships and sharing power for decision making requires trust. In communities where many adults had negative experiences with schools and schooling, educators must work even harder to develop that trust.

in some cases were removed from families by court order (e.g., children who were sent to live in treatment centers, moved to many different schools due to foster care, or Native Americans who were sent to government-run facilities for re-education). Events held in school buildings often evoke discomfort, such as feelings of anger or inferiority, for adults who have suffered such negative experiences. Other adults might have experienced condescension or rebuffs by school officials as they made earlier attempts to interact as parents with school staff.

First-time parents, even those with successful school experiences, are learning about being parents and interacting with the school system in an entirely new way. Most schools will have some engaged family members who are comfortable cooperating as partners with educators. As a start, these are good people to involve, but in the long term, those who feel marginalized or uncomfortable with schools and school people will need representation.

Overcoming barriers to effective family engagement requires understanding three constructs that influence parents' engagement: (1) personal motivators—how parents describe their role as a parent ("role construction") and how confident they feel about their ability to help their children ("efficacy"); (2) whether parents feel invited by both school staff and their own children ("sense of invitation"); and (3) the school's responsiveness to family-life variables such as parental knowledge, time and energy, and culture (Hoover-Dempsey et al., 2005; see also www.vanderbilt.edu/Peabody/family-school/model.html). The process of bringing together schools and families, especially those families that are marginalized or harder to reach, involves welcoming parents and other adult family members, respecting and affirming any type of involvement a family member chooses, and helping both school staff members and family members to focus on the child and connecting on common areas of interest that contribute to a child's education (Mapp, 2003).

TEN TRUTHS ABOUT PARENT INVOLVEMENT

The National Parent Teacher Association (PTA, n.d.) synthesized much of the research about family involvement into the following "10 Truths About Parent Involvement." These truths offer a foundation on which to build a strong partnership between families and schools.

1. All parents have hopes and goals for their children.

2. Parents differ in their abilities and/or resources to help their children reach those goals.

3. The parent is the central contributor to a child's education.

4. Parent involvement must be seen as a legitimate element of education and deserves equal emphasis with elements such as school improvement and evaluation.

5. Parent involvement is an ongoing process, not a series of events.

6. Parent involvement requires a shared vision, policy, and framework for planning programs and practices that are connected to student learning.

7. Many barriers to parent involvement are found within school practices, attitudes, and assumptions.

8. Successful parent involvement programs help families guide their children's learning from preschool through high school.

9. Families from diverse backgrounds have their own set of norms and experiences that often influence their relationship with schools.

10. Parents are more likely to become involved when

   o They understand that they *should* be involved.
   o They feel *capable* of making a contribution.
   o They feel *invited* by the school and their children.

A number of these truths are covered in other parts of this chapter, but two stand out as factors in creating long-lasting, positive relationships between schools and students' families that can lead to positive student outcomes. Number 5 notes that family involvement is an ongoing process, not a series of events. The role of organized parent leadership groups (e.g., PTAs, PTOs, HSAs) is often defined as fund-raisers and event planners for the school community, with little or no involvement from school leadership. Consequently, opportunities to strengthen collaboration between families and demonstrate connection between family engagement and student success at school are lost. The last "truth," which captures why parents get involved, highlights the importance of building trusting relationships between families and schools.

PTA's National Standards for Family–School Partnerships

School and parent leaders who are serious about improving partnerships among home, school, and the community could use the national PTA's standards as the basis for planning how families, schools, and communities should work together to support student success (see Figure 3.1). To help facilitate the implementation of programs and policies that are guided by the standards, the national PTA (2009) also developed an implementation guide that provides specific goals for each standard and indicators for measuring whether the goals are being met.

Figure 3.1   PTA National Standards for Family–School Partnerships

---

Standard 1. Welcoming All Families Into the School Community

Families are active participants in the life of the school, and feel welcomed, valued, and connected to each other, to school staff, and to what students are learning and doing in class.

Standard 2. Communicating Effectively

Families and school staff engage in regular, two-way, meaningful communication about student learning.

Standard 3. Supporting Student Success

Families and school staff continuously collaborate to support students' learning and healthy development both at home and at school, and have regular opportunities to strengthen their knowledge and skills to do so effectively.

Standard 4. Speaking Up for Every Child

Families are empowered to be advocates for their own and other children, to ensure that students are treated fairly and have access to learning opportunities that will support their success.

Standard 5. Sharing Power

Families and school staff are equal partners in decisions that affect children and families and together inform, influence, and create policies, practices, and programs.

Standard 6. Collaborating With Community

Families and school staff collaborate with community members to connect students, families, and staff to expanded learning opportunities, community services, and civic participation.

Source: PTA, 2009, p. 6.

TYPES OF PARTNERSHIPS/INVOLVEMENT

Students' families are not homogeneous with respect to their interest in engaging with schools. A continuum exists in most schools, from very engaged adults who are advocates for children, show up at meetings, and are vocal, to those who are invisible to the school. Yet, as Henderson and Mapp (2002) discovered,

Families of all cultural backgrounds, education, and income levels encourage their children, talk with them about school, help them plan for higher education, and keep them focused on learning and homework. In other words, all families can, and often do, have a positive influence on their children's learning. (p. 34)

This is not to say that all families encourage their children. Differences in culture, education level, or economic circumstances sometimes affect involvement but do not keep concerned and caring adults from wanting to be partners in their children's education.

Differences in culture, education level, or economic circumstances sometimes affect involvement but do not keep concerned and caring adults from wanting to be partners in their children's education.

One type of partnership involves serving on advisory councils or decision-making bodies. This type of partnership tends to address specific populations of students and usually has opportunities and interest for only limited numbers of adult family members. For many, their desire for partnership is at a more individual level: partnering for their own children's success. On an individual level, partnering involves open communication and joint decision making about an individual student's education. The individualized education plan (IEP) teams, which are required for students with documented disabilities by the Individuals with Disabilities Education Act (IDEA), are an example of joint decision making around educational goals and the means for achieving them.

When a family has a student with a disability, it makes the partnership between the family and the school even more complex. The same is true for students with mental or physical health issues that affect their education (and all of their life). Some educators have suggested that all students would benefit from an IEP. Open communication might include e-mail notes from teachers about assignments, concerns, and progress, and—in the other direction—notes from adult family members about family resources that could contribute to lessons, needs for accommodation, and help with questions while engaging in homework.

Joyce Epstein (1995) has categorized family involvement with schools into six types of involvement:

1. *Parenting:* "Assist families with parenting and child-rearing skills, understanding child and adolescent development, and

setting home conditions that support children as students at each age and grade level. Assist schools in understanding families."

2. *Communicating:* "Communicate with families about school programs and student progress through effective school-to-home and home-to-school communications."

3. *Volunteering:* "Improve recruitment, training, work, and schedules to involve families as volunteers and audiences at the school or in other locations to support students and school programs."

4. *Learning at home:* "Involve families with their children in learning activities at home, including homework and other curriculum-linked activities and decisions."

5. *Decision making:* "Include families as participants in school decisions, governance, and advocacy through PTA/PTO, school councils, committees, and other parent organizations."

6. *Collaborating with the community:* "Coordinate resources and services for families, students, and the school with businesses, agencies, and other groups, and provide services to the community."

Epstein's six types of involvement demonstrate that everything does not flow from the school to the family. There is reciprocity, which is a form of partnership or collaboration. The National Network of Partnership Schools at Johns Hopkins University (n.d.) defines decision making as "a process of partnership to share views and take action toward shared goals for school improvement and student success, not a power struggle" (n.p.).

These types of involvement acknowledge that schools alone cannot and should not attempt to meet all students' needs and that "family engagement is a shared responsibility in which schools and other community agencies and organizations are committed to reaching out to engage families in meaningful ways and in which families are committed to actively supporting their children's learning and development" (Weiss & Lopez, 2009, n.p.).

MOVING FROM PARENT
INVOLVEMENT TO PARENT ENGAGEMENT

Being involved is important—a necessary but not sufficient condition for the success of children in school. A parent can be involved by attending meetings, but the relationship is not likely to move to the level of collaboration until *engagement* happens. Engagement takes the collaborative relationship to a more meaningful level. A person who is engaged has a vested interest in all parts of the process, understanding the system and his or her place in it.

In an exploration of family engagement, Fette and Glimpse (2008) found that families defined it as an active, ongoing process that facilitates opportunities for all family members to participate and contribute in all decision making for their children, engaging in meaningful involvement with specific programs and with each other. This family-driven definition of family engagement flows from the family to the school and back.

Fette and Glimpse (2008) discovered that family engagement was a process moving either toward increased partnership between families with children or retreating from that goal. They looked for what families found to be engaging versus what they did not, and for patterns that led away from communication and collaboration. With those findings, they sought to recognize factors early in the process that could help families and schools identify their strengths and what was getting in their way. The two main factors contributing to family engagement, they found, were (1) families being valued and (2) communication.

Family engagement cannot happen if families do not feel valued as a part of a system in which they are active participants. Families bring a unique perspective and deep knowledge of their child that comes from living with them day to day; they are valuable contributors to children's success. When families are part of all discussions and solutions in a child's life, they are invested in the entire education process and buy into their part of the solution.

Communication is woven through all aspects of family engagement. It begins with professionals listening to the views of family members and keeping active, ongoing, and open lines of clear communication. Both school staff and family members must value communication and collaborative problem solving as well as goal setting. Families must feel comfortable voicing their concerns and sharing their goals. They need to see their concerns and goals incorporated into their child's day-to-day experience. The most effective family–school partnerships occur when schools have created a welcoming climate where trusting relationships between parents and teachers are developed and where meaningful, two-way communication is focused on student success.

True engagement brings families into leadership roles. The Harvard Family Research Project (HFRP) and the National PTA developed a policy brief on the role of school districts in promoting family engagement (Westmoreland, Rosenberg, Lopez, & Weiss, 2009). This paper includes examples of bringing families into leadership roles in school systems. It examines how six school districts created and sustained family engagement within the educational system. The findings highlight three core components of effective family engagement: creating districtwide strategies, building school capacity, and reaching out to and engaging families. The policy brief recommends the following ways in which federal, state, and local policies can promote district-level family engagement efforts that support student learning:

- Create an infrastructure for districtwide leadership in the area of family engagement.
- Build district capacity for family engagement through training and technical assistance.
- Ensure reporting, learning, and accountability for family engagement.
- Help districts understand, design, and implement strong evaluation strategies.

In the six school districts studied, districtwide strategies included

- Leadership from the district;
- Tracking data on family participation;
- Inclusion in the school improvement plan; and
- Having family and community involvement coordinators and district-level steering committees.

School capacity-building included

- School-based parent liaisons;
- Professional development for principals and teachers;
- School-based family engagement teams;
- Data coaches who helped schools use a parent satisfaction survey to set school improvement goals;
- Hosting parent observation days, including rubrics for family engagement in self-assessment tools;
- Hosting parent-to-parent opportunities; and
- Sharing learning at school staff meetings.

Examples of how these schools and districts reached out to and engaged families included

- Creating parent academies that involved training on being an advocate for one's child;
- Initiating specific activities that engaged fathers in non–sports-related events such as classroom observations and checking backpacks for homework assignments;
- Actively communicating through phone calls and weblogs;
- Visiting community gathering places;
- Creating radio messages;
- Home visitations by school staff;
- E-mail messaging;
- TV programming for parents;
- Surveys and focus groups; and
- Regular meetings of the superintendent with parent and community groups. One of the key points of the HFRP/PTA policy brief is the importance of administrators, educators, parents, community members, and policy makers understanding that family engagement is a shared responsibility.

The school districts referenced in the brief were medium to large in size but diverse in school population and location within the United States. They demonstrated promising practices that other school systems could use to start similar programs. The types of collaboration they exhibited provide models for districts already working to engage families, as well as for districts seeking to implement total stakeholder involvement in improving outcomes for student learning.

ACCOMMODATING SPECIAL NEEDS

All school districts have students with special needs. Disabilities are a natural part of life and affect a great number of students. Meeting the needs of students with disabilities requires strong collaborative partnerships among students' families, service providers, and the schools.

Several federal laws as well as state regulations cover children and youth who are eligible to receive special education services. The federal laws with the most relevance to schools with respect to students with disabilities are the Individuals with Disabilities Education Act, the Rehabilitation Act of 1973, and the Elementary and Secondary Education Act of 1965 (reauthorized in 2001 as the No Child Left Behind Act). IDEA guides the ways in which states, school districts, and public agencies provide early intervention, special education, and related services to more than 6.5 million eligible infants, toddlers, children, and youth with disabilities. The Rehabilitation Act of 1973— a civil rights law prohibiting discrimination on the basis of disability— existed before IDEA. Section 504 of this act continues to play an important role in education, especially for students with physical disabilities, and served as a foundation for the development of the Americans with Disabilities Act. The Elementary and Secondary Education Act is the nation's general education law; it places considerable emphasis on equalizing education for disadvantaged students. Some other relevant laws are the Family Education Rights and Privacy Act (FERPA), which governs the confidentiality of students' educational records and parental rights for access to such records, and the Freedom of Information Act (FOIA).

The laws governing the education of a child with a disability are complex and often confuse both schools and students' families. Good communication and true partnerships among schools, students' families, and sometimes service providers can make these laws work for the benefit of students with disabilities. When everyone works together, they are more likely to learn, understand, and implement the necessary services for any given child. In the absence of solid partnerships and good communication, the relationships can become contentious and sometimes involve legal action.

> *When everyone works together, they are more likely to learn, understand, and implement the necessary services for any given child.*

REVISING THE SCENARIO

Going back to the original scenario, what might Principal Stevens have done differently? First, consider the problem (obesity) broadly, and approach it as an issue for which many different people and agencies have responsibility. Seek partners such as community coalitions concerned about obesity or cardiovascular risks or diabetes management. If such coalitions exist, the school should be a partner, which could relieve some of the school's burden.

Next, identify people who should be at the table when planning a course of action. Consult with the school nurse about any parents who might have expressed concern or interest in the issue, and seek ways to involve them in planning an initiative. School leaders might also identify interested school staff (such as those in food services, physical education, and school nursing), as well as students with an interest in this important issue.

A planning group that includes parents, school faculty and staff, and community members at all levels could perform some needs assessments that would consider both what the school could do and is doing and what students' families and others in the community could or should be doing. The needs assessment should examine the economic realities of families in the school, known dietary restrictions, and the ethnicities represented in the community. Part of the needs assessment might include identifying resources available in the community, the school, and among families. Many parents have expertise that they might be willing to share with the school. Any plans should include communication strategies that take into account the languages spoken in the home. The plan should be multifaceted, involve not only schools and families but also relevant community groups, coordinate with other initiatives that involve partnerships, and consider both short-term and long-term concerns and solutions.

Such collaboration is likely to continue long enough to achieve results, reduce the burden on the school, take advantage of resources, bring family members into leadership roles and tap into them as experts, and ensure that all stakeholders feel invested and take the actions needed to achieve success in school for every student.

CONCLUSION

When families, community members, and teachers and other school staff all work together to support the academic success of all children, everybody wins. Teacher morale and job satisfaction improve; respect for the teaching profession increases; communication among family members, teachers, and school administrators increases; more community support becomes available; and, most important, student achievement and quality of life improve.

True partnership is a two-way street, with both partners contributing and benefitting. Such partnership does not occur without intentionality, mutual respect, and excellent communication. While educators, policy makers, and others continue to seek new and different ways to improve educational outcomes for children and youth, effective family–school partnerships must be part of the solution.

REFERENCES

Epstein, J. (1995, May). School/family/community partnerships: Caring for the children we share. *Phi Delta Kappan, 76*(9), 701–712.

Fette, C., & Glimpse, C. (2008). *Family Engagement Model.* Presented at 13th annual Advancing School Mental Health Conference, Phoenix, AZ. Retrieved July 30, 2009, from http://sharedwork.org/16507/files/?bydate=1.

Henderson, A. T., & Mapp, K. L. (2002). *A new wave of evidence: The impact of school, family, and community connections on student achievement.* Austin, TX: Southwest Educational Development Laboratory. Retrieved July 11, 2009, from http://www.sedl.org/connections/resources/evidence.pdf.

Henderson, A. T., Mapp, K. L., Johnson, V. R., & Davies, D. (2006). *Beyond the bake sale: The essential guide to family–school partnerships.* New York: The New Press.

Hoover-Dempsey, K. V., Walker, J. M. T., Sandler, H. M., Whetsel, D., Green, C. L., Wilkins, A. S., et al. (2005). Why do parents become involved? Research findings and implications. *Elementary School Journal, 106*(2), 105–130.

Mapp, K. L. (2003). Having their say: Parents describe why and how they are engaged in their children's learning. *School Community Journal, 13*(1), 35–64.

National Network of Partnership Schools, Johns Hopkins University. (n.d.). "Epstein's six types of involvement: Decision making." Retrieved July 11, 2009, from http://www.csos.jhu.edu/p2000/nnps_model/school/sixtypes/type5.htm.

PTA. (2009). *PTA National Standards for Family–School Partnerships: An implementation guide.* Chicago: Author. Retrieved August 25, 2009, from http://www.pta.org/Documents/National_Standards_Implementation_Guide_2009.pdf.

PTA. (n.d.). *10 truths about parent involvement.* Retrieved July 20, 2009, from http://www.pta.org/Documents/10_Truths_About.pdf.

Weiss, H., & Lopez, M. E. (2009). Redefining family engagement in education. *Family Involvement Network of Educators (FINE) Newsletter, 1*(2). Retrieved July 11, 2009, from http://www.hfrp.org/family-involvement/publications-resources/redefining-family-engagement-in-education.

Westmoreland, H., Rosenberg, H., Lopez, M. E., & Weiss, H. (2009, July). *Seeing is believing: Promising practices for how school districts promote family engagement* (Issue Brief). Cambridge, MA: Harvard Family Research Project. Retrieved July 30, 2009, from http://www.hfrp.org/publications-resources/browse-our-publications/seeing-is-believing-promising-practices-for-how-school-districts-promote-family-engagement.

CHAPTER FOUR

THE "WHAT" AND "HOW" OF HELPING PARENTS HELP STUDENTS BECOME SUCCESSFUL LEARNERS

YONI SCHWAB AND MAURICE J. ELIAS

W hen we speak to groups of teachers or parents at a school, we often ask them, "How many of you think it's important that your school work hard to ensure that your students are knowledgeable?" Not surprisingly, nearly all the hands go up. "How about responsible?" Again, many hands go up. "How many of you want the schools to help children resolve conflicts nonviolently?" Hands shoot up quickly. "And what about be caring?" Just about all the hands are up. "How about drug free?" Every hand goes up strongly.

"Well, our schools are very busy," we respond then. "There is so much they have to accomplish, and they can't do everything.

Knowledgeable, responsible, nonviolent, caring, and drug free. Let's say the school board said they could not focus on all of these; you have to give one up. Which one would it be?"

A highly animated conversation typically follows. When parents are pressed, most will give up knowledgeable, though they are not happy to do so. However, the alternatives seem far worse. "It is good," we tell them, "that you don't want to give up caring because, when you retire, no matter how smart your kids are and how much money they make, if they aren't caring, you won't see a dime."

Parents and teachers have a good laugh, but they walk away realizing that students can't become successful learners if we only strive to make them knowledgeable without also focusing on their social-emotional and character development (Elias, Bryan, Patrikakou, & Weissberg, 2003). Equally clear to parents is that this goal is best reached through a partnership of schools and parents.

In our over 40 combined years of research, clinical practice, teaching, and school intervention, one of the most important lessons we have learned is that the "what" we want changed is always more obvious than "how" we make the change happen. Whenever someone acts as a change agent (and good teachers and school administrators always aspire to that role), it is much easier to advocate that some particular content be changed—be it a curriculum, a policy, or a school culture—than it is to figure out the process of changing it. How often do the most noble and unimpeachable interventions fail because we do not have a process to make the changes stick?

The "what" we want changed is always more obvious than "how" we make the change happen. It is much easier to advocate that some particular content be changed—be it a curriculum, a policy, or a school culture—than it is to figure out the process of changing it.

Promoting children's social-emotional and character development is certainly no exception. While research has already discovered a lot about what those practices look like, the process of changing teachers' and, especially, parents' practices to match is infinitely more difficult. We need to apply every facet of our own social and emotional intelligence—from perspective taking to communication to problem solving—to help other adults help children.

Decades of research have consistently demonstrated that children's healthy social-emotional and character development (SECD) is critical not only for their ability to function as citizens; it is also inseparable from their academic and vocational achievement. So, although the primary mission of schools is academic, they ignore SECD at their peril (Elias, 2009).

The inverse is true of parents. A critical component of parenting is fostering academic success through, for example, communicating a high family value on education, speaking with children about the world around them, reading to children, and establishing an appropriate environment for study and homework. However, parents' primary mission is to foster their children's social-emotional growth so that they can become caring, respectful, responsible, individuated, and satisfied adults.

Schools, therefore, can be more successful, in terms of both academic and social-emotional outcomes, when they help parents foster social-emotional and character development in their children in an emotionally intelligent way. Of course, schools and parents have extremely limited time and resources to make this happen, so the first emotional skill to apply is *focus*. Schools must focus on one, two, or—at most—three things they want parents to do and then reinforce them repeatedly over time. Having multiple programs, each with its own theme, is not productive.

This chapter has two parts: the "what" and the "how." First we describe, in brief, the top three SECD themes (the "what") that we think are critical for parents if they are to support their children's success in school. While there are dozens of social-emotional skills to choose from, we shall prioritize these three. Then we address some of the principles and ideas for "how" to help parents change. That, of course, is the greater challenge.

"WHAT" SHOULD SCHOOLS HELP PARENTS TO CHANGE?

The most important part of choosing a focus for any program of parent education or outreach is that you choose something and then stick with it over multiple programs and even over multiple years. Just as students do not learn to read in a single evening or even in a single year, parents cannot be expected to learn how to parent in a way that fosters SECD in a shorter time frame. An assessment of the needs and interests of the parents in your community is a valuable starting point to begin to develop your outreach. Here are three broad SECD themes in which parents should develop competencies. However, it is important to make a long-term commitment to whatever you decide to emphasize.

Emotional Literacy and Decision Making

The core foundational social-emotional skill is the awareness and regulation of emotions. Picture the children in your school who are able to recognize and manage their own emotions as well as recognize and respond appropriately to the emotions of others. Now picture those who do not have those skills. That distinction likely differentiates the star students and citizens from the ones who are constantly in trouble or in the nurse's office. Research has even shown that, compared with academic success in elementary school, a child's level of SECD in elementary school is a better predictor of academic success in middle school (Caprara, Barbaranelli, Pastorelli, Bandura, & Zimbardo, 2000).

Emotional literacy begins with being able to *name* emotions. When children can name how they feel and communicate that appropriately, as in an I-message (e.g., "I feel really frustrated and disappointed that I lost the basketball game"), they are halfway to managing them. Parents should learn to use emotion words with their kids, especially boys. (Parents tend to use fewer such words with boys.) When reading to children, it is important for parents (as well as educators) to focus on the emotions in pictures and help children learn how a raised eyebrow, an upturned mouth, a hunched-over posture, a furrowed brow, or mouth and eyes wide open are among many signals of emotions. They should label strong emotions—from happiness to anger to fear—when they see them, and ask their kids how they feel when something good or bad happens. Parents can also learn to label feelings in others when they speak to their children as a way to help them understand what motivates others and to build empathy.

The use of emotional language at home facilitates parents' teaching children emotion-management strategies. Parents can learn to teach their children to breathe slowly, to relax their bodies like a wet noodle, to relax muscle groups using visualization, to count to 10, to walk away and get a drink before acting, and even to talk themselves out of anger or frustration or sadness. Many parents already attempt to teach these social-emotional skills, but they make one cardinal error. They try to teach them when they are most urgently needed: when the child is upset. However, we humans learn new things very poorly when we are emotionally distressed. Besides, even if they could learn, children (and adults) are rarely receptive to these sorts of strategies when they are seeing red. It is critical to teach, practice, and reinforce these skills when children are calm. Then, parents can cue them to use their well-learned skills when they are *beginning* to get upset.

Parents are often reluctant to speak to their children about difficult situations or mistakes they have made because our society tends to shy away from unpleasant emotions. We have the unrealistic goal of everyone feeling happy all the time. We hope that all will be good if we just, in the words of Johnny Mercer, "accentuate the positive and eliminate the negative." Many parents, furthermore, fall into the trap of trying to protect their children from every sort of hurt and frustration. Unfortunately, this is incredibly counterproductive. If children are protected from all unpleasantness and pain, they will never learn that they can handle them.

This misstep is a major contributor to problems with anxiety. Many parents give in to their children's anxieties, never urging them to face their fears. In the short run, the child is more comfortable. In the long run, the child never learns to conquer fear-provoking situations, which leads to a life of anxious misery. For example, every preschool and kindergarten teacher has seen children who are anxious about separating from a parent. When parents give in to this common fear by staying in the classroom for hours or even taking their child out of the program, the anxiety is reinforced. However, when parents teach their children to identify and manage their fears, and children are pushed to separate, that fear typically abates very quickly.

Emotional literacy and self-regulation allow for effective problem solving, which is another social-emotional skill under this heading that parents can learn to teach their children. Parents can learn to scaffold their children's decision making by sitting with them and facilitating the child's—not the parent's—finding a solution. Using questions, they can prompt their children for their feelings in relation to the problem and the feelings of others involved. They can brainstorm solutions and ask which one the child plans to use. (The important part here is to not judge the child's choice, unless the solution is dangerous or completely unacceptable.) They can rehearse the solution and then follow up with the child to hear how effective the solution was (Elias, Tobias, & Friedlander, 2000). This type of problem-solving conversation gives the parent an opportunity to teach related skills, such as respectful, assertive communication and delaying gratification.

Encouraging Children

All parents want their children to do well and to feel good about themselves. Despite their good intentions, parents need guidance in

All parents want their children to do well and to feel good about themselves. Despite their good intentions, parents need guidance in encouraging their children to do the right thing and to genuinely feel confident about their abilities.

encouraging their children to do the right thing and to genuinely feel confident about their abilities. Two common pitfalls abound. The most obvious is when parents put down, yell at, or belittle their children. Most parents do this because they lose control when they themselves are frustrated, tired, and overwhelmed, and this is almost unavoidable in today's hectic, pressure-packed culture. Most parents don't feel good about these reactions but also find themselves falling into the trap of repeating them. This leads them to feel both disappointment in their children and disappointment in themselves. Because this has become a habit, it is not as easy to change as school personnel might think. (Of course, the same thing applies to teachers who scold or put down their students.) There is also a subset of parents who actually use these negative tactics intentionally, based on the misguided belief that they will motivate their children and make them tougher. (Need we say that there is a subset of similarly misguided educators?) The less obvious pitfall is when parents attempt to praise and be positive in unproductive ways. However, we will address the more obvious pitfall first. Though we will explore alternatives to yelling as a behavior-management tactic later in this chapter, the first step is to improve the relationship between parent and child. The quality of that relationship has a powerful influence on the child's social-emotional development.

Increasing Positive Interactions

The antidote to negative interactions is to help improve the tone of the parent–child relationship. The quality of this relationship has a strong influence on children's SECD. While this can be a difficult area for a school to have a substantial impact, we have found that there are some strategic emphases that can catalyze an unexpected degree of change in parents and help them develop an underlying feeling of respect and warmth toward their children. If children fundamentally feel that they are understood by their parents and cared about, conflicts and even yelling are less likely to negatively affect social-emotional development.

The first step is to increase the ratio of positive-to-negative interactions. John Gottman (1979, 1994) discovered that strong couples have four or five positive interactions for every negative one, while couples headed for divorce have an even ratio of positive to negative. That finding has been extended to adult–child interactions; when adults and children have at least a 5:1 ratio of positive-to-negative interactions, the relationship is stronger, and the child's behavior and emotional development both benefit (see Friman, Jones, Smith, Daly, & Larzelere, 1997). Positive interactions can include praise, hugs, smiles, concerned questions, and any other kind of warm interaction. This is a challenge for many parents who, in their frustration, give a steady stream of angry redirections and criticisms. It is easier for parents to increase the rate of positive-to-negative interactions if they can identify and cherish strengths in their child while developing empathy for the child's daily challenges. Ultimately, parents must learn to respect the child for what he or she can do and view difficulties as challenges that they can help the child to manage or overcome.

In order for parents to accomplish this task, they need to be able to stop themselves when they are so frustrated that they want to yell and retaliate against their children. There are a few ways to help parents with this daily struggle. One approach we have found successful is to use the activity in Table 4.1 during parent workshops, or even during meetings with parents. As the procedure shows, this helps parents become more aware of how they are actually expressing their feelings toward their children. Another approach is to help parents appreciate their children's strengths and have empathy for their challenges. Parents can be educated about childhood development so that their expectations of their children are not exaggerated. Teachers can also send notes and e-mails to parents about when children are being successful and spend time during parent conferences emphasizing children's strengths. Parents can also learn to recognize their own personal frustrations, whether those have to do with their jobs or their relationships with a spouse or friend, and not take them out on their children. Teaching parents to cope more effectively with stress and anger can help them to take a moment and respond thoughtfully when their children do something that angers them. Like their children, they can learn social-emotional skills, such as slow diaphragmatic breathing, progressive muscle relaxation, self-talk, and counting to 10. Mindfulness techniques can help parents cope with anger and stress as well as help them notice how they naturally react to problems. When they are mindful, they can respond more thoughtfully.

Table 4. 1   Emotional Expression: Examine Your Pattern and Range

How often do you display the following feelings toward your children?

	Always	Regularly	Once in a While	Rarely	Never
Love	1	2	3	4	5
Pride	1	2	3	4	5
Fun	1	2	3	4	5
Compassion	1	2	3	4	5
Respect	1	2	3	4	5
Understanding	1	2	3	4	5
Interest	1	2	3	4	5
Anger	1	2	3	4	5
Disappointment	1	2	3	4	5
Frustration	1	2	3	4	5
Annoyance	1	2	3	4	5
Embarrassment	1	2	3	4	5
Anxiety	1	2	3	4	5
Withdrawal	1	2	3	4	5

Note. We list positive feelings first because many people forget about these. What is the balance between positive and negative feelings you show—not what you feel, but what you show? (You can also ask your spouse how he or she would rate you, and you can ask your teenager the same question, if you are brave enough.) Remember, our children only know what we show them. Parents tend to think they show more positives than they actually do because they *feel* more positives, but are quicker to show the negatives. So most parents find they need to put more emphasis on showing more of the positive feelings because the negatives seem to come out fairly easily. The key for our children is *balance.* Put your focus on the positives, and don't worry so much about decreasing the negatives at the moment. The latter is hard for most parents. You can rebalance through positives.

Adapted from *Raising Emotionally Intelligent Teenagers* (Elias, Tobias, & Friedlander, 2002).

Parents also need to learn the importance of self-care in the quality of their parenting. If parents do not get appropriate nutrition, sleep, and exercise, they are more likely to be vulnerable to frustration and to resort to unproductive parenting techniques. This message can be delivered, for example, during Family Health Night programs. This can be an occasion to give the message to parents who center their lives on raising their children that, just as in the use of oxygen masks on an airplane, they must take care of themselves first. Enjoying their own adult lives, contributing to the community, and giving adequate attention to their romantic relationships are critical for the quality of their parenting in the long run. Though they may pay a little less attention to their children, they will be happier and less stressed when they are with their children, and they will provide a healthier, well-rounded model for their children, both of which are crucial for social-emotional health. Schools can give parents ideas for self-care that are economical and time-efficient and remind them that this work is just as important to their children's health as it is to their own.

Effective Praise

Just being positive is not enough, however. Even when parents are positive with their children, there are ways this behavior can be counterproductive for the children's social-emotional growth. Carol Dweck and her colleagues have consistently shown in their studies that praise focusing on the child's traits can, counterintuitively, undermine a child's self-confidence (Mueller & Dweck, 1998). Take the example of a child who does well on a math test, and the parent says, "Wow, you must be very smart." If the child does not do well the next time, research shows, the child might logically conclude that she is no longer smart. Children who receive this type of "trait-based" praise tend to enjoy tasks less, persist less, and be more interested in comparing scores than in learning how to improve their performance. The opposite is true for children who hear praise for effort. In the math test example, if the child received the praise, "Wow, you must have worked very hard," the outcome tends to be quite different. If the child performs poorly the next time, she is likely to conclude that she did not work hard enough, and she will try harder. Students who learn to think about intelligence as unmalleable and consider every performance a referendum on their intelligence become anxious and avoid challenges. The need to put in effort comes to be viewed as a sign of low ability. However, when children link their performance to effort and mastery as opposed to some fixed trait, this incremental view of intelligence motivates them to take on challenges in order to strengthen their "brain muscles." While most parents would never tell their children that they are dumb, ugly, or bad, telling them that they are smart, beautiful, and good can have, paradoxically, the same undesirable effect.

Deci, Koestner, and Ryan's (1999) research has challenged another ostensibly positive parent intervention: rewards. When rewards (and even praise) are viewed as controlling, they can undermine internal motivation. In a classic study, when children were told they would be rewarded for drawing with magic markers, they were less likely to use magic markers afterward during free play than before they were rewarded. Though tangible rewards can influence behavior when they are available, the child's behavior tends to return to baseline—or even below baseline—when and where the rewards are not available. Why is this a problem? Healthy social-emotional development implies that children internalize pro-social values over time and can motivate themselves to act autonomously in line with their values and (healthy) societal norms. If the rewards and praise used by parents undermine children's autonomous performance of these important behaviors, then what have we accomplished? Parents should learn about the types of rewards and praise that, though potentially effective in the moment, interfere with that development.

The alternative, according to Deci et al. (1999), is to give feedback that maximizes the information to the child about his or her actions while minimizing the perception of control. In order to accomplish this, positive feedback is best when it is delivered immediately after the action is performed and is unexpected. When feedback is expected, the child may simply be working for the reward and, therefore, would only perform it again when the reward is available. In general, tangible rewards should be avoided, if possible. They carry a greater likelihood of feeling controlling, and they can distract from the actual behavior being targeted. (This is why kids in so many "caught being good" programs are more focused on being caught than being good.) Praise should be genuine and measured,

Positive feedback is best when it is delivered immediately after the action is performed and is unexpected. When feedback is expected, the child may simply be working for the reward.

not fake and disproportionate to the accomplishment. Children do not take seriously praise that is condescending or over the top—and they do not tend to respect or even like adults who give such praise. Praise should also be specific and, where possible, provoke internal judgment rather than external. Rather than the ubiquitous, meaningless, and dismissive "Good job!" parents can learn that it is far more affirming and useful to thoughtfully describe a child's drawing, ending with a question such as, "What do you think?" or "What are you going to add next?"

In sum, verbal praise that is focused on effort rather than on the child's "traits," that provokes internal judgment, that is specific, that is unexpected, and that is respectful and genuine can boost a child's confidence and motivation while enhancing the parent–child relationship. Unfortunately, praise and rewards of the opposite types can, over the long term, have the opposite effects. Schools will find that workshops focusing on appropriate use of praise and rewards, and maintaining a focus on these techniques until they become ingrained, will pay many dividends for both parents and educators.

Setting Limits Effectively

The third vital SECD topic for parents is setting and enforcing limits. Children will not deploy their social-emotional skills consistently—even if they are loved, encouraged, and well-taught—if they are not aware of family and societal rules and the consequences that come with violating those rules. Even if children have the ability to act appropriately, without rules and consequences, they inevitably figure out that they can satisfy their desires more expediently by violating others' rights and acting recklessly. Rules and consequences can provide the motivation necessary to use the skills they have learned. Ultimately, however, those rules and consequences must help children to internalize the behaviors and values that they represent so that they continue to act pro-socially when they are not being monitored. Our way of life relies upon good citizenship from most people most of the time, despite living in a relatively free society, because they have internalized the values behind the laws, not simply because they fear being caught. Living by rules and experiencing consequences when the rules are violated are the basis for learning self-control.

Rules

Rules define the basic parameters for children's behavior. Parents can learn how to make clear, consistent family rules that fit their children's developmental levels. These rules, and the reasons behind them, should be discussed as a family—and not only in the heat of the moment, when a rule has been violated. Children do not need to agree with the rules, but knowing parents' reasons for them helps to give kids insight into adults' problem-solving process. Some rules, like respecting others, need to be role-played and rehearsed in order to be followed consistently because they are difficult to accomplish. Ideally, children can contribute to making and modifying the rules, which is empowering and motivating, though parents should always feel comfortable having the final word. The consequences for breaking the rule should also be clear from the outset so that children can begin to think through the consequences of tempting misbehaviors, even before they perform them.

Though firm and consistent rules are vital, they should not be too narrow. Western societies over the past generation or two are unique in that adults spend much more time with, and give much more direct supervision to, their children. Not too long ago—and to this day in many places—even young children spent much time outside playing and exploring without close adult oversight. This gave them many opportunities to try out different behaviors and to learn from mistakes. Children learned how to manage and avoid conflicts through the natural social order. There are serious drawbacks and dangers inherent in this system, but it does give children ample opportunity to develop independent life skills. When parents supervise children at all times, they tend to try to manage their behavior much more actively. They give redirections and limits constantly (though they do not always follow through if commands are ignored). These narrow limits do not give children sufficient freedom to test things out and learn from their own mistakes. Allowing children to try and fail in relatively safe, developmentally appropriate ways is an indispensable part of learning social-emotional skills.

In summary, rules must be clearly delineated to children along with a rationale. They should be regularly discussed, revised, and even rehearsed, in order to keep them fresh and clear in children's minds. Finally, wherever possible, clear consequences for violating rules should be laid out in advance.

Consequences

Consequences are vital not only to keep children safe and to modify troublesome behavior, but also to teach self-control and help children internalize the values behind good behavior. If children do not experience the consequences of their actions, their social and emotional skills are never solidified. However, many parents are reluctant to discipline their children or confused about how to do so. Too many parents yell, nag, warn repeatedly, lecture, argue, embarrass, and punish haphazardly—none of which helps children to develop the cause-and-effect thinking they need.

Parents can learn that there are three basic features of responses to misbehavior that nearly all experts agree are vital to effectively respond to misbehavior. First, parents must consider in advance the consequences for common and not-so-common misbehaviors so that, when misbehavior inevitably occurs, the parent is ready. Thinking ahead also helps parents to anticipate and thereby prevent many problems.

Second, parents must remember to be specific and very predictable about the consequences they select. Once they set a limit or threaten a consequence, they *must* follow through. Children test adults with misbehavior in order to see how reliable and trustworthy they are. It is as if they are conducting science experiments: If adults are not predictable and consistent, the children do not respect or trust them. This requires parents to learn to warn once, then act, rather than warning a dozen times and getting so frustrated that they lose control. Robert MacKenzie (1998) calls this "the dance." When parents cut off debate early and simply dictate a consequence, children learn that they cannot argue indefinitely and hope to wear the parent down. Children who are accustomed to inconsistent parenting often seem shocked when they are punished, because they are never quite sure if they should take all the repeated warnings seriously.

Third, parents must learn to deliver consequences respectfully. This includes explaining the rationale for the rule and the consequence and maintaining a matter-of-fact tone of voice. Many frustrated parents find this to be exceedingly difficult. However, frequent yelling loses its effectiveness, disrupts the parent–child relationship, and can even reinforce negative behavior. It also models poor management of emotions and poor interpersonal problem-solving skills. Parents who can learn to prepare for problems, to be consistent, to give a consequence after minimal warnings, and to deliver consequences respectfully are likely to be successful in gaining their children's compliance and fostering social-emotional development.

In addition to these three basic tenets (on which nearly all experts agree) for delivering consequences, we suggest that there is another vital element that is somewhat more controversial. The *content* of the consequences is a key element in promoting the internalization of appropriate behavior and values. External, unrelated consequences—like some forms of rewards and praise, as described above—can undermine internal motivation. Natural and logical consequences, appropriately delivered, mimic the real-world consequences for misbehavior as much as possible; as a result, they help the child to generalize appropriate behavior to new settings, especially those in which no adults are present to set limits. Natural consequences are defined as consequences that occur because of the natural order of things. For example, if a child plays roughly with a toy, and the toy breaks, the loss of the toy is a natural consequence. The parent's role is simply to avoid replacing the toy or even saying, "I told you so"—both of which undermine the simple and eloquent lesson.

While natural consequences are ideal, in many situations they are unrealistic. The natural consequence for walking in the street is to be hit by a car. So, when the natural consequence of a misbehavior is too severe or if the behavior affects others in a significant way, a logical consequence can be used. These are consequences carried out by adults that attempt to mimic the real-life consequences as much as possible. Logical consequences have three features: They must be respectful, reasonable, and related. *Respectful* refers to the way in which the consequence is delivered. Consequences that are given in a calm, matter-of-fact way are taken more seriously than those delivered in anger. High emotionality on the part of the parent only provokes that type of response from the child, which distracts from the lesson to be learned. (Of course, it also can be reinforcing to a child looking to push a parent's buttons.) *Reasonable* implies that the magnitude of the consequence is relatively small. Small consequences for small misbehaviors are ideal and tend to minimize the need for larger misbehaviors that would call for more dramatic consequences. Early intervention with a small consequence, such as removal from the location of the misbehavior for 3 minutes, is reasonable and often effective, and it obviates the need for drastic action later.

The most defining feature of logical consequences is that they are *related* to the misbehavior. Ideally, they involve fixing the problem, such as cleaning up spilled juice. When that is not possible, they try to mimic the adult consequences that come with an analogous behavior. For example,

The most defining feature of logical consequences is that they are related *to the misbehavior. Ideally, they involve fixing the problem, such as cleaning up spilled juice.*

if an adult does not finish his work at the office, he may need to finish it at home instead of relaxing or watching TV. Similarly, if a child does not complete his homework, he may need to complete it the following night and miss out on some activity or free time. If a driver speeds through an E-ZPass checkpoint (an electronic toll-collecting station) numerous times without slowing down, the driver's E-ZPass device may be taken away temporarily. Similarly, if a child is throwing a ball around the house and endangering the furnishings, the ball should be taken away temporarily. In neither case would it be "logical" for the child to be grounded or to go to bed without dinner. Parents who learn to use logical consequences help their children to learn the natural outcomes of their behavior, which helps them understand when and why to employ their social-emotional skills.

One might focus on many different topics in parent education and outreach. The three suggested here—building social and emotional skills, effectively encouraging children, and setting limits—are at the core of social-emotional growth and functioning. They are also basic and broad enough to provide a framework for many specific topics, from Internet safety to bullying. However, there are many other topics that schools may choose to focus on when addressing parents. The important thing, as previously stated, is to stick with one, two, or three themes over time. Whatever theme is chosen, the next section explores ideas for educating tired and busy parents using inevitably limited school resources.

"How" Can Schools Help Parents to Change?

The three broad SECD topics we presented as priorities for parents are challenging, but they are also accessible. Countless books, articles, and Web sites have addressed these topics. The greater challenge, and the one that is rarely discussed, is "how" to help parents change. In the preceding portion of this chapter, we have embedded the core principles that we believe schools should be invested in conveying to parents. As we have also suggested, however, the delivery system for these sound ideas is another matter.

The main principles of effective parental learning are the same as learning in any other setting:

- The goals should be focused and clear.
- The choice of topics should be based on an assessment of the students' (in this case, the parents') needs and desires.
- The motivation for learning (indeed, even for just showing up) must be at the center of the planning.
- Terms and concepts must be explained clearly and reviewed until they are mastered.
- Skills should be specific, not general, and broken down into their component parts. They must then be modeled and taught directly and sequentially.
- Learning must be interactive, multisensory, and supportive of different learning styles.
- Teaching should be parent-focused; that is, it should take the perspective of the parents' learning and their cultural backgrounds.
- Creative activities and engaging discussions that are enjoyable and emotionally evocative will be best remembered.
- There must be opportunities to practice and review the skills learned using, for example, role-playing.
- Learning should always be as active as possible.
- Finally, the educational program must be evaluated for effectiveness.

The most effective process of parent education begins long before a lecture or a meeting is advertised. In order to maximize effectiveness, relevance, and buy-in from parents, they must be involved in every step of the process. The first step is to recruit a steering committee that comprises both school representatives and parents. Having parents' input from the beginning in how parent outreach is conducted is critical to success. In addition to providing vital information about parents' interests, schedules, and so forth, parent volunteers can be the leaders in recruiting parents to participate in the programs. Recruiting members from the school's parent–teacher and home-schooling associations or organizations is important to both support and strengthen those groups and to provide a mechanism for gleaning representative input from parents.

The second step is to define the focus of the parent education. This may begin with an assessment of what parents need and want to learn. Parent surveys are a great way to determine parents' interests. It is best to give parents short surveys to complete when they are a captive audience, such as when they attend back-to-school night or parent–teacher conferences. While surveys over the Internet provide an easy solution, in some communities they may systematically exclude those who might be most in need, so they should be used with caution. (That said, note that there are free survey Web sites, such as www.SurveyMonkey.com to help you create your surveys.)

After the survey has been completed, workshop topics can be tailored to parents' predominant concerns, which will also serve to motivate participation. In fact, parent education can be offered through a variety of modalities, in addition to the more typical "workshop" approaches; these are outlined in Table 4.2. Coming up with creative programs and formats, and then advertising them in an attractive manner, will always be essential for optimal success. Building programs around outside speakers, a book club, a video screening, or a presentation by children all help to improve attendance. Regardless of format, for a topic to be effective it must be a long-term theme, not a one-time experience. Follow-up steps must be laid out at the time of the initial event, and means of access for those missing the first event but wanting to get on the bandwagon should be made clear. These follow-up steps can be facilitated by post-event publicity in school letters, on school Web sites, in notes to parents, and in stories placed in local newspapers or on town Web sites. (This can be a great project for high school students doing service learning or studying mass media.)

There are many different ways to collect state-of-the-art information on a given SECD topic. The committee, under the guidance of professionals with expertise in social-emotional concerns (such as school psychologists, social workers, and guidance counselors), can research the information itself. It can also reach out to consultants and speakers with expertise in SECD. Because effective intervention typically requires multiple opportunities to learn in different modalities, multiple avenues of information gathering should be pursued.

Table 4.2   Suggested Avenues for Educating Parents

In-Person	Remotely	Broader Community Support
• Workshop with school professional or outside expert • Back-to-school night • New parent orientation • Parenting discussion groups • Parent–teacher association (or similar organization) events • Parent–teacher conferences • Student performances and celebrations • School athletic practices and competitions • Commencement	• Newsletters (paper and electronic) • Brochures (paper and electronic) • Web site • Blogs • Internet discussion boards • Social networking sites • Existing school–home communication, such as report cards, mailings, and e-mails • DVDs and CDs of speakers and student presentations • Podcasts and streaming audio and video • Videos on the school cable station	• Town government • Local press • Community Web sites • Pediatricians • Local businesses

Once the steering committee identifies a focus for the parent education, it must develop a series of modalities with which to communicate the chosen theme. Traditional workshops in the school, delivered by school personnel or outside speakers, can be valuable. However, if the goal is to share this theme across as much of the school community as possible and not just the minority of gung-ho parents who always attend workshops, then this modality is not sufficient. It must be augmented with a series of both in-person and "remote" education modalities.

In-person programs are typically more engaging (and probably more effective) for those who attend. The challenge, of course, is to get busy, overloaded parents to show up. Workshops and other events should be held at a variety of times so that they are convenient for a variety of schedules. Some parents are available during school hours, some in the evening, and some only on weekends. Whenever possible, provide food and babysitting, which make it far easier for parents to attend. Many parents are more likely to attend school workshops that hold some benefit for them beyond simply improving their parenting. Here are a few ideas for piggybacking on existing events that may already attract parents to the school:

- If there is a new "big theme" in the school, such as learning social-emotional skills, then back-to-school night may be a great time to introduce it to the parents.
- Similarly, the new parent orientation program, if there is one, can be a useful vehicle for communicating the schoolwide themes to new families.
- Discussion groups on parenting can be formed; these can meet in the school or in parents' homes.
- The parent–teacher association (or a similar organization) can help to organize events or allocate space at existing events to address the theme.
- On parent–teacher conference evenings, an area of the school can be set up with information about the parent-education theme. Information in this area can be passive (that is, posters to read or videos to watch), or it can be active, with someone ready to describe the initiative and engage parents in learning about it.
- Student performances and celebrations can be a creative vehicle for communicating the parent-education theme, particularly if the theme is integrated with programs for the students. For example, if the theme is resolving conflicts, students can put on a performance about this theme for parents. This not only motivates parents to attend, but it also encourages students to take ownership of the theme.
- School athletic practices and competitions can be particularly good opportunities to engage fathers. For example, fathers (and mothers, too, of course) can be invited to assist with coaching, where the parenting themes are discussed and modeled. This can be a particularly effective way to involve fathers in parenting education, according to pilot studies (Fabiano, 2007).

- Commencement, when parents and students are feeling proudest of the school, can be an opportunity to address the theme and congratulate everyone on their progress while challenging them to continue to grow in that area.

When holding these or other workshops, be sure to distribute handouts and take-home materials so that parents can continue to digest the information. Handouts can be cues to try a new skill. Make video recordings of events available to parents who are not able to attend, either by placing DVDs in the school library or sending them home with the students, broadcasting the videos on the school's cable channel, or streaming or podcasting them on the school's Web site.

"Remote" learning modalities are those that do not require parents to show up, meaning the learning happens at home. An effective parent campaign combines both in-person and remote activities. This is useful not only for parents who do not attend the workshops and events; it can also be an excellent cue and reinforcement for parents who do attend. Newsletters and brochures, both paper and digital, are the most basic form for conveying the parent-education theme home. The school's Web site can also be a useful modality. The Web site can have traditional text pages but also blogs with opportunities for comments, as well as audio and video podcasts. Podcasts can include recordings of speakers who have visited the school, information gleaned from other sources, and (if you really want parents to watch) presentations created by the students themselves. Online social networking and discussion groups can also be used for this purpose. With some help from committed parents, these can be used to create a "buzz" around the topic. Existing parent–teacher communications, from registration packets to weekly e-mails to report cards, can contain information on the theme.

An effective parent campaign combines both in-person and remote activities. This is useful not only for parents who do not attend the workshops and events; it can also be an excellent cue and reinforcement for parents who do attend.

Addressing the theme beyond the school community can have a very powerful effect. The theme could be town- or districtwide and incorporated into communitywide events. The town or municipal government, local press, and community Web sites could be engaged in supporting the theme and disseminating information. Pediatricians can be useful consultants and allies in educating parents. Local businesses can sponsor events or activities and post information.

Learning new parenting skills is challenging. No matter what modality you choose, always assume a low rate of retention of information. It is vital to avoid the one-time workshop, whose information is rarely referred to again. Change rarely happens in that context. Information must be repeated across multiple modalities and over time—even years. One way to address this issue is to consider the material to be a curriculum that requires scope and sequence. Ask yourself, "What do we want parents to learn and do over the 3–6 years that their children are in our school?"

CONCLUSION

We have collected these ideas for reaching busy parents over time, but there are many more possibilities out there. Creativity, knowing the community, and engaging parents in the planning from the beginning are key ingredients to overcoming the obstacles to parent education. We have suggested three broad themes for educating parents to promote social-emotional and character development in their children: emotional literacy and decision making, encouragement, and setting limits effectively. Whether you choose any of these themes, or different ones, the keys are careful selection based on parents' expressed needs and persisting with whatever theme is chosen over the long term. Infusing the school community with the theme and engaging parents in many different ways offer the best chance to change behavior and to help children grow into the responsible, nonviolent, caring, drug-free, and yes, knowledgeable people we hope that they will become.

REFERENCES

Caprara, G. V., Barbaranelli, C., Pastorelli, C., Bandura, A., & Zimbardo, P. G. (2000). Prosocial foundations of children's academic achievement. *Psychological Science, 11*(4), 302–306.

Deci, E. L., Koestner, R., & Ryan, R. M. (1999). A meta-analytic review of experiments examining the effects of extrinsic rewards on intrinsic motivation. *Psychological Bulletin, 125*(6), 627–668.

Elias, M. J. (2009). Social-emotional and character development and academics as a dual focus of educational policy. *Educational Policy, 23,* 831–846.

Elias, M. J., Bryan, K., Patrikakou, E., & Weissberg, R. P. (2003). Challenges in creating effective home–school partnerships in adolescence: Promising paths for collaboration. *School Community Journal, 13*(1), 133–153.

Elias, M. J., Tobias, S. E., & Friedlander, B. S. (2000). *Emotionally intelligent parenting: How to raise a self-disciplined, responsible, socially skilled child.* New York: Three Rivers Press.

Elias, M. J., Tobias, S. E., & Friedlander, B. S. (2002). *Raising emotionally intelligent teenagers: Guiding the way to compassionate, committed, courageous adults.* New York: Three Rivers Press. (Out of print; available from the author at RutgersMJE@aol.com and in Spanish at www.amazon.com)

Fabiano, G. A. (2007, November). Adapting behavioral parent training approaches for fathers of children with ADHD. In A. Chacko (Chair), *Behavioral parent training for ADHD: Next steps for difficult-to-treat and difficult-to-engage families.* Symposium conducted at the meeting of the Association for Behavioral and Cognitive Therapies, New York.

Friman, P. C., Jones, M., Smith, G., Daly, D. L., & Larzelere, R. (1997). Decreasing disruptive behavior by adolescent boys in residential care by increasing their positive to negative interactional ratios. *Behavior Modification, 21*(4), 470–486.

Gottman, J. M. (1979). *Marital interaction: Experimental investigations.* San Diego, CA: Academic Press.

Gottman, J. M. (1994). *What predicts divorce?* Hillsdale, NJ: Erlbaum.

MacKenzie, R. J. (1998). *Setting limits: How to raise responsible, independent children by providing clear boundaries* (2nd ed.). Roseville, CA: Prima Publishing.

Mueller, C. M., & Dweck, C. S. (1998). Intelligence praise can undermine motivation and performance. *Journal of Personality and Social Psychology, 75,* 33–52.

CHAPTER FIVE

FAMILY LITERACY

The Roles of School Libraries and Public Libraries

LESLEY S. J. FARMER

A key factor in the literacy of our young people is the involvement of parents and guardians. No matter what the culture, parents are generally considered their children's first teachers. Yet sometimes these adults simply don't know how to get involved in their children's education. They may not know what role is appropriate, or they may not have the skills needed to help their own children. As the need for adult literacy becomes ever more vitally important, these issues of parent involvement become even more complex and problematic.

Because librarians work with the entire community, and network with other local community entities, they are well positioned to help facilitate family literacy. Libraries have traditionally provided a lifetime's worth of reading that supports literacy. While public libraries typically offer preschool programs, helping young children become reading-ready, the usual notion is that the schools should be responsible for teaching reading when those same young people enter formal education. The public library's literacy effort is then thought to resume once the student enters the "real world" beyond academia,

———————— ————————

Both school and public librarians know that neither party can provide all the literacy services that are needed. The real issue, therefore, is how to build a successful partnership based on a clear understanding of each librarian's role.

typically through adult education and family literacy initiatives. Yet both school and public librarians know that neither party can provide all the literacy services that are needed. The real issue, therefore, is how to build a successful partnership based on a clear understanding of each librarian's role.

This chapter identifies factors that influence parental involvement and describes ways in which school and public librarians can help parents gain the skills needed to support the literacy efforts of their families.

INTRODUCTION

The sight of parents bringing their children to the public library delights librarians. They see parents as the first models of lifelong learning. When children first scribble their names on a library card, librarians smile—and hope that library habits take root and blossom.

Too often, however, parents do not hold their children's hands to walk them to the school library. In some areas of the United States, children may not even see a school library until high school. Even with a good school library, most parents think that school is not the same free, independent space as a public library. Some parents may feel uncomfortable in school settings because they themselves lack formal education or cannot read. Moreover, unfortunately, some schools do not encourage parent involvement. How sad! For with proper guidelines and training, parents can serve as strong educational partners. And for those parents who frequent other types of libraries, the school library can reinforce and expand the library's role as cultural preserver and educational haven for the community. Particularly in light of the importance of family literacy, libraries can provide valuable services to parents and guardians (in this article, the term *parents* is used to describe both parents and guardians), as well as develop meaningful partnerships with them in order to help the whole family succeed.

WHAT IS FAMILY LITERACY?

The term *family literacy* refers to family members—both adults and children—learning and practicing literacy skills together. Family literacy emphasizes informal, lifelong learning that can happen every day: in preparing meals, in shopping, in working, or in participating in religious experiences. As parents read directions or explain to a child how to perform a process, literacy skills are being learned.

The U.S. Congress defined adult literacy in the 1998 Adult Education and Family Literacy Act as "an individual's ability to read, write, and speak in English, compute and solve problems, at levels of proficiency necessary to function on the job, in the family, and in society." Head Start, Even Start, Reading Is Fundamental (RIF), and Title I all exemplify federal literacy programs that incorporate family involvement. Those funded programs state that family literacy programs need to entail adult basic education, early childhood education, parenting education, and literacy-centric parent–child interaction.

Family literacy programs are initiated outside the family unit, usually by a social agency, e.g., schools, libraries, or recreation centers. These groups address family and community literacy needs and tend to focus on ways in which adults can become more involved in their children's education by giving them the tools to be successful, such as reading tutoring, strategies for reading aloud, and tips on selecting reading material. Family literacy programs often meld early childhood and adult education, offering opportunities to strengthen parent–child relationships. They also provide child-centric and adult-centric activities that motivate all ages to become more literate.

No one set of activities can be said to constitute a family literacy program. Projects may range from family storytelling sessions to vocational workshops, from book donations to newborn children to Family Reading Nights, from individual tutoring to computer-based instruction, from family literacy programs for the incarcerated to help for teenage moms. Likewise, the geographic scope can range from one church group to an international organization such as the International Reading Association (Sapin, Padak, & Baycich, 2008).

In terms of library involvement, public libraries tend to be the main type of library to offer family literacy programs because their mission is to serve the reading needs of the entire community. School libraries may provide services through parent-teacher associations (PTAs) or school-related adult education initiatives. Community college libraries are beginning to get involved as adults go back to school to fill in gaps in their education. The National Center for Family Literacy has a Family Literacy–Community College Initiative that targets community college students; the center offers them family literacy programs as a way to encourage lifelong education.

WHO IS THE PARENT POPULATION?

From teenagers to baby boomers, from single moms to extended families, from foster caregivers to stand-in grandparents, from *Mayflower* descendants to newly arrived green-card holders, from illiterate adults to honorary doctors, from the homeless to empire builders—the parents or guardians of today's students represent a vast spectrum of skills and experiences. They differ widely in socioeconomic background and available resources—whether material, psychological, or time-related.

Regardless of their differences, parents have in common certain knowledge, needs, and expectations. Parents bring to the learning table their intimate knowledge of and emotional connection to their children. As they encourage and support their children, parents provide examples of good teaching. Because they know how their children learn, parents can optimize instructional strategies. Parents themselves need to feel needed and secure. Many wish to improve themselves, and all wish to be recognized for their efforts for their family or for themselves.

For their part, children share certain expectations about their parents. According to Galinsky's (2001) research, children want their parents to enjoy their jobs, but also to have time for their family. Youngsters need to be heard and nurtured by both mothers and fathers. As librarians recognize the needs of families and the potential benefits of working with them, all parties can learn from each other and contribute to student success.

THE ROLE OF THE SCHOOL LIBRARY

The school library can play a unique role in helping and supporting parents and can make good use of their involvement in family literacy. The school library serves the entire school community. It is the information center across the curriculum, and it provides recreational reading and viewing for all.

Although all librarians strive to educate their users, the school librarian is uniquely trained as a teacher in addition to his or her skills of librarianship. Possessing an overview of the school's curriculum and educational purpose, the school librarian provides resources and services that support literacy. The school librarian works with classroom teachers to design meaningful lessons that draw upon available resources to engage students and to formally and informally instruct them in literacy skills. Especially as schools emphasize more resource-based learning, literacy learning activities become valuable core strategies.

The other focus of a school librarian's expertise is the clientele. Because students use the library regularly, the school librarian develops a professional and individual relationship with each of them. Even students who don't use the library get to know the librarian because they share the same building and school culture. With this knowledge, the school librarian can, and should, offer valuable literacy assistance to parents as well as to the public librarian.

Nevertheless, school libraries may not be the first place that parents consider as a source of family literacy services. The traditional relationship in schools is between teacher and student: Teachers communicate with their students daily and in depth, and contact parents only as needed in relation to students' work. School librarians tend to work with students throughout their time at the school, but have little contact with parents—or school librarians may enjoy a close professional relationship with parents even after their children graduate.

To make the most of parental involvement in school libraries, librarians need to ascertain the literacy needs of both students and parents and what library services fit those needs. Moreover, they need to take the initiative in entering the parents' world—be it through individual classroom teachers or PTAs. One of many tasks for librarians is

> *To make the most of parental involvement in school libraries, librarians need to ascertain the literacy needs of both students and parents and what library services fit those needs. Moreover, they need to take the initiative in entering the parents' world.*

to identify the key social structures where parents tend to congregate and get information. Fortunately, this kind of outreach is made easier by such technologies as desktop publishing, Web sites, and community-based television broadcasting.

In terms of family literacy programs, school librarians need to solicit administrative approval for any initiatives. Usually, the school itself establishes such programs, and the library can contribute in several ways to the school's success, for example, by

- Providing developmentally appropriate resources, from kindergarten through adult;
- Creating bibliographies and "webliographies" of appropriate reading materials and family literacy resources;
- Providing tips on selecting and using resources to support family literacy;
- Conducting workshops on family literacy topics, particularly reading activities;
- Sponsoring reading tutoring and other literacy programs in the library;
- Permitting families to read together in the library; or
- Hosting family literacy events such as Family Reading Nights and parent–child book clubs.

THE ROLE OF THE PUBLIC LIBRARIAN

What does the public librarian contribute to this mix? A broad perspective that embraces the entire community. Because the public library serves all ages and interests, its collection offers rich breadth as well as depth. Its diversification helps families because it offers picture books for pre-readers of all ages as well as sophisticated treatments of complex issues for the reading scholar. Because the public library is not constrained by a school philosophy, it can offer a greater variety of materials to match the leisure and recreational interests of a diverse population. Moreover, because the collection is open to all, little stigma is attached to the sometimes surprising reading choices of family members.

Another major factor that distinguishes the public library from the school library is time. The library is usually open during the evening and on weekends. There are no "passes," no discipline-based supervision, no artificial bells or "pass time" (except for closing time). Possibly most important, families normally make a conscious choice to visit the public library, so they are not a captive audience. True, for some youngsters, teacher-set deadlines and grades may be the motivating factors rather than pure love of reading, but still, a certain amount of control rests in the hands of every library patron, which translates into a more liberated, positive attitude. In addition, the public librarian usually deals with the user on a one-to-one basis rather than as a whole class, so family members have a good chance of getting personalized attention with fewer arbitrary time limits.

With regard to family literacy programs, public libraries have a substantial range of programming efforts that have met with success. Representative efforts include

- Book give aways;
- Activities that promote reading (puzzles, word games, storytelling);
- Literacy tutors;
- Instruction in English;
- Small-group reading and writing sessions;
- Computer learning labs;
- Field trips;
- Orientation to library and community literacy resources and services;
- Workshops and mini-courses on literacy activities, child development, parenting, health issues, and basic adult education;
- The hosting of family literacy events;
- Side-by-side activities for parents and children;
- Pre-reading activities training; and
- Databases and referrals to community services (Nickse, 1989).

WHAT'S WRONG WITH THIS PICTURE?

Both types of librarians—public and school—are motivated to support family literacy initiatives. But problems can arise, often resulting from lack of communication. Politically, the public librarian usually bears the brunt of the family literacy responsibility. If one kind of library is going to be eliminated, it is likely to be the school library. If staffing is reduced dramatically, that reduction is likely to translate into keeping just a school library clerk while a professional handles the public library.

In terms of users, few members of the public visit school libraries, but *everyone* goes to the public library. Rarely does the public librarian say to a patron, "It doesn't matter that we don't own that book; you can always go to the school library to read it." However, a similar phrase is repeated all too often by teachers and school librarians as they conveniently refer a student to the local public counterpart.

Occasionally, the public library sponsors family literacy programming, or hosts an event that could interest the school community—but fails to contact school librarians. Because the public librarian is often not familiar with the schools' curriculum or teachers' timelines, he or she may not realize that the author Louis Sachar will be visiting the public library during the same week that Mrs. Jones's class is reading Sachar's novel *Holes*. Likewise, if school librarians do not tell public librarians about summer reading lists or adult education offerings, the public library may find that its resources fall short of meeting unanticipated demands. If the school and public librarian do not communicate regularly, golden learning moments may be lost.

BUILDING RELATIONSHIPS

Family literacy efforts can provide an excellent opportunity for librarians to improve their relations with their local counterparts. In responding to the following inventory, librarians can mark those items that merit more time and effort in order to strengthen professional contacts and provide better family literacy support.

- Do you have a list of local school, public, government, and special libraries? Do you know their librarians? Have you contacted them and introduced yourself?
- Do you communicate regularly with local librarians?
- Do you communicate about literacy efforts?
- Do you exchange library holdings lists of periodicals, indexes, special collections, or non-print items? Do you create districtwide lists of these resources?
- Do you exchange family literacy booklists or instructional aids, either librarian- or teacher-generated?
- Do you help other librarians with their collection development related to family literacy through reviewing, exchanging, donations, group purchasing, or collection specialization?
- Do you publicize a variety of family library activities?
- Do you schedule joint programming—sharing speakers, displays, equipment?
- Do you tell users about family literacy opportunities at other libraries?

- Do you share professional materials or conference insights about family literacy?
- Do you train other librarians or facilitate group professional development about family literacy?
- Do you support all family literacy issues, such as school campaigns or federal programs?

The preceding model of collaboration also applies to library relationships with community family literacy groups. Do libraries have a directory of community institutions and organizations—business service groups, local government agencies, educational sources, volunteer groups, nonprofit organizations, youth programs, and recreational centers?

How many of these kinds of groups support family literacy? These are also potential community partners that can be cultivated. Besides offering valuable resources, community groups are credible channels of communication, often to parents who could benefit from family literacy programs. Here are some ways in which librarians can create positive relationships that can foster mutual support:

Besides offering valuable resources, community groups are credible channels of communication, often to parents who could benefit from family literacy programs.

- *Build on existing structures.* If librarians have an established tie with local family literacy programs, they can talk with their administrators to see if they can serve as liaisons to such program sponsors.
- Develop a local *family literacy list* of those community agencies. This is an easy way to make a connection with them and promote their services to parents.
- *Speak* at local family literacy sponsor groups about the role of libraries.
- *Instruct* local youth groups, such as Scouts and the 4-H.
- *Provide* background information about family literacy for a community agency as appropriate, such as the reading interests of preschoolers.
- *Seek sponsorship* from the community for family literacy events or contests, such as the donation of coupons for free food as prizes in a reading contest.

- *Display* community family literacy efforts in the library.
- *Host* family literacy community speakers in the library.
- *Contact* local media channels, such as newspapers and broadcast community programming, urging them to communicate information about family literacy.
- *Participate* in local community family literacy activities—book discussion groups or parenting classes, for instance (and wear a library T-shirt!) (Bajaly, 1999).

These ties work both ways. As librarians become more connected members of the community, they come to know more about the various areas in which families live—and they can better serve them as a result.

BARRIERS TO PARENTAL PARTICIPATION

Whether it be an individual librarian or a consortium, librarians also need to identify the barriers that can operate to prevent full parental participation in family literacy programs in library settings. Parents control some of these factors; agencies control others. Still other factors are controlled by outside forces. Examples of such barriers follow.

- *Parental personal issues:* These include home demands, personality, negative past experiences with schools or libraries, conflicting values, health issues, or even fear of the unknown. Librarians need to ensure that the library has a safe and supportive feeling so that parents feel comfortable seeking assistance.
- *Parents' low expectations of libraries, their children, or themselves:* Probably the best antidote to these feelings is concrete evidence of success. Thus, the more that librarians can document students' reading achievement or progress in literacy, the more parents can believe in their children and libraries. Similarly, the more librarians can train parents to help their children at home and at school, the more parents gain in self-confidence and transfer that feeling to their relationships with their children.
- *Students' attitudes about parents:* Sometimes, older children might not want their parents to be highly visible or close at hand. Libraries can contact parents behind the scenes about

family literacy projects. Remote access via the Internet, available at any time, allows parents to participate in family literacy activities far from the critical (or embarrassed) eyes of their children.

- *Logistics such as transportation, day care, lack of resources, language barriers:* As much as possible, librarians need to work with schools or other public agencies to explore ways of overcoming such obstacles. Solutions may include carpooling, cooperative babysitting arrangements, translators, and loans of equipment.

LEVELS OF INVOLVEMENT

Most parents really do want their children to achieve in school and in life. Research demonstrates the powerful influence of parents and guardians on their children's academic performance in general, and on literacy specifically. However, parents may not always know the best way to help their children, nor are they always clear about their own relationship to the entire educational process. Over the years, numerous researchers (in particular, Epstein, Coates, & Salinas, 1997) have identified five major levels of parent involvement:

1. *Family obligation:* maintaining a healthy home environment for learning;

2. *Involvement* at school or in the library (possibly as a volunteer);

3. *Home education/literacy:* monitoring student homework and communicating high expectations for student achievement in literacy;

4. *Decision making and advocacy* at school or the library through governing bodies and associations; and

5. *Community collaboration,* as a liaison with the school or library and in support of family literacy.

Each of these levels is appropriate and helpful. The question is how to ensure that parents can be supported to the extent that they wish to become involved in family literacy programs. Specific examples of library services at each of the five levels of parent involvement follow.

Family Obligation

Librarians can communicate ways for parents to provide a reading-friendly atmosphere at home through the use of newsletters, voicemail messages, online tips, presentations at PTAs and service groups, Open House displays, and workshops. They can also show parents how to set up a workable computer corner—say, a table in a corner of a room that can serve as a handy work station. Librarians can help parents select good reading materials for their children and also provide good adult material (including resources on parenting) for parents to borrow and read at home, thus modeling good habits for their children. Librarians can also offer parents workshops on special skills such as reading aloud; storytelling; and activities to reinforce reading such as retelling stories, fingerplay, rhyming and other word games, nursery songs, word searches, and clipping newspapers. In this technological age, librarians can also provide guidelines and sponsor technology fairs for choosing computer systems and Internet service providers.

Volunteering

Parents can provide volunteer service to the library or family literacy programs in myriad ways. Some may do a single project or event, whereas others may work on a weekly basis for years. Some may contribute by answering the telephone or checking in workshop participants, whereas others may spearhead major fundraising campaigns. Some may enjoy the stability of one clear-cut task; others may prefer a variety of tasks. Some may work at the front desk; others may contribute as "virtual" volunteers online. The librarian's main task is to match family literacy services with parental interests and capabilities, always remembering to provide adequate training, supervision, and recognition.

Home Education/Literacy

Librarians can teach parents about family literacy through publications, videotapes, Web tutorials, workshops and presentations, and as part of volunteer training. They can display students' literacy efforts in the library or on the Internet so parents can know what level of performance to expect from their children. Librarians can also provide parents with information about literacy events, such as a schoolwide

"Read a Million Pages" campaign, so parents can encourage their children to participate. In some cases, parents may not even understand the concept of libraries, either school or public, so librarians may need to orient them to the library's services and point out the library values of free and confidential access to information and other reading resources. If parents have difficulty reading, librarians can help them find adult literacy programs or sponsor a program on site. For the technologically illiterate, hands-on workshops to develop computer comfort would be most welcome. Librarians can also help parents with Internet issues of concern and use this opportunity to make Internet use a family event rather than a protectionist campaign.

Decision Making and Advocacy

Librarians should seek parental participation on family literacy committees. With telecommunications, parents can be "virtual" members and even join in discussions online. On the other hand, librarians should make sure that parents without the means to own computers can either borrow them or have equitable access to them. Similarly, librarians need to be sensitive to parents' own reading challenges, providing oral means of communication where necessary.

Community Collaboration

Parents can be powerful family literacy spokespersons. As librarians build good working relationships with parents and keep in regular communication with them through the Internet and other channels, they can call on these supporters to build the library's case relative to family literacy within the community and also encourage other parents to take advantage of the library's many and diverse offerings.

WORKING WITH PARENTS

To work successfully with parents, librarians need to acknowledge the characteristics of adults as learners and educational partners. Parents have

- A rich repertoire of experience to build on and use as input;
- Strong existing habits, so a major emphasis must be on facilitating change;

- Self-interest, so services must appeal to parents' interests and needs;
- Limited time, so training and tasks need to be done efficiently;
- Social needs, so time for interaction should be built into the schedule;
- A need for results, so learning should be concrete and easily applied to daily life;
- A need for self-confidence, so learning should be safe and paced for success.

Barber, Barakos, and Bergman (2000) and Berger (1995) provide specific tips for involving parents in the library's family literacy program:

- Develop a list of possible family literacy tasks, indicating the skills needed to perform them.
- Develop a volunteer application form asking for information about skills, interests, availability, and personal references.
- Interview parents to determine their fit and to clarify expectations.
- Train for each task; provide guidance (coaching, manuals, tutorials), supervision, correction, and development.
- Communicate and evaluate regularly; build a team approach to family literacy.
- Recognize both effort and results; support and nurture parents' growth; and know when it is time for them to move on.

Some of the specific ways in which parents can help include

- Performing clerical duties;
- Technical assistance;
- Storytelling and reading aloud;
- Tutoring and reading assistance;
- Publishing and design work;
- Telecommunications;
- Videotaping, downloading, and duplicating;
- Assisting with displays and artwork; and
- Providing financial assistance.

In a busy library, parent peer coaching should also be encouraged so that mutual support teams can flourish. Sometimes parents participate for social reasons and stay because they learn so much, and others find that they gain new friendships along with the literacy skills they had hoped to gain from the start.

When parents benefit from a library's family literacy programs, they can model positive behavior and help teach their children more effectively at home and at school. The entire family becomes empowered.

CONCLUSION

Although at first glance it may seem that the library is going an extra mile or two in providing family literacy services for parents and opportunities for their involvement, such outreach actually forms a core part of the library program because it positively affects reading and supports the development of a learning community. When parents benefit from a library's family literacy programs, they can model positive behavior and help teach their children more effectively at home and at school. The entire family becomes empowered, and the library itself becomes a more powerful force for community development.

No one institution can address all of the varying literacy needs that families bring to the library desk. However, the whole is certainly far greater than the sum of its parts when school and public librarians work together to satisfy family literacy needs. Independently, the two institutions might well fall short of success, but when both types of libraries build on mutual interests, families and libraries can build on each other's strengths and provide well-rounded family literacy programs based on knowledge about informational and recreational reading resources as well as knowledge about each other's libraries.

REFERENCES

Bajaly, S. (1999). *The community networking handbook.* Chicago: American Library Association.

Barber, J., Barakos, L., & Bergman, L. (2000). *Parent partners.* Berkeley, CA: Gem.

Berger, E. (1995). *Parents as partners in education* (4th ed.). Englewood, NJ: Prentice Hall.

Epstein, J., Coates, L., & Salinas, K. (1997). *School, family, and community partnerships: Your handbook for action.* Thousand Oaks, CA: Corwin.

Galinsky, E. (2001). What children want from parents—and how teachers can help. *Educational Leadership, 58*(7), 24–28.

Nickse, R. (1989). *The noises of literacy: An overview of intergenerational and family literacy programs.* Washington, DC: Office of Educational Research and Improvement.

Sapin, C., Padak, N., & Baycich, D. (2008). *Family literacy resource handbook.* Kent: Ohio Literacy Resource Center.

CHAPTER SIX

BALANCING YOUR COMMUNICATION LEDGER

*Using Audits to Involve Communities
and Build Support for Schools*

EDWARD H. MOORE

W e talk; they listen. In essence, this is what school communication is all about. Right?

Hardly.

While the stereotypical trappings of school communication—brochures, newsletters, Web sites, and so on—might typify traditional, one-way communication tactics, they don't represent the full potential that two-way communication offers schools. Planned, regular, two-way communication is essential to building the kind of strong working relationships and active engagement essential to school success and student achievement.

The implication is this: Successful school communication is as much about people as it is about things. "Things" in communication (those publications, Web sites, and more) are vital, of course. But the efficacies of communication programming should not be judged

To be effective, school communication needs to generate both information and *involvement. It needs to build both understanding* and *prompt action.*

on the simple fact that certain "things" were produced and distributed. Rather, communication programming should be judged on exactly what people *did* as a result of being exposed to it. In other words, to be effective, school communication needs to generate both information *and* involvement. It needs to build both understanding *and* prompt action.

A TWO-WAY PROCESS

Public relations researchers, practitioners, and scholars have long advocated building communication efforts that foster dialogic processes. "Public relations is much more than the one-way dissemination of informational materials. It is equally important to solicit feedback" (Wilcox, Ault, Agee, & Cameron, 2000). If successful communication is about talking and listening, then effective educational communication must tap into the real power inherent in the process. That is, it must involve stakeholders in meaningful, two-way exchanges of ideas and information.

In a two-way, symmetrical model of public relations, according to public relations scholars Jim Grunig and Todd Hunt (1984), communication does not attempt to change merely the orientation of audiences. Rather, communicators work to influence the ways in which the organization and its audiences jointly orient with one another. As an essential part of my preparation for this chapter, I interviewed a number of top-notch professionals in the field of communications and school public relations. Some of the information was gathered in the form of written responses to questions, and in other cases personal interviews were conducted in May 2009.

The definition of educational public relations used by the National School Public Relations Association (NSPRA, 2002) notes, "It relies on a comprehensive, two-way communication process involving both internal and external publics with the goal of stimulating better understanding of the role, objectives, accomplishments, and needs of the organization" (n.p.).

One benefit of this involvement is that it ensures a better understanding of what the community wants, both now and in the future. It strengthens cooperation with organizations and individuals throughout the school system's various communities. In addition, it helps to foster the use of educational offerings—further tying schools to the communities they seek to serve (Bagin, Gallagher, & Moore, 2008).

But finding meaningful ways in which constituencies can engage with a school system can be difficult. Involvement efforts that are unplanned or poorly managed can produce more discord than harmony. *The challenge is this:* How might a school system, with limited human and fiscal capital, hope to boost involvement and bolster its communication effectiveness? Here is one good solution: the communication audit.

MULTIPLE TACTICS

Communication audits combine a number of research and involvement tactics to complete a thorough programmatic assessment of communication activities throughout a school system (Moore, 2008). Generally, a communication audit provides an in-depth, independent review of school communication programs. School systems can conduct audits using their own resources, but because the process also can play an important role in involving the community and school families in both the communication process and the planning for that process, external auditors can be important in establishing validity and reliability for the process and its findings. Professional organizations such as NSPRA (www.nspra.org), as well as communication consultants, offer audit services for their members and clients.

The assessment aspects of a communication audit can help school systems make the most cost-effective deployments of their communication resources. Audits can be used to identify meaningful outputs in existing programming and to quantify performance benchmarks for future programming. However—and this is important—because audits reach out to the community for input and guidance, they can also, when undertaken as part of a transparent process, set the stage for creating meaningful community involvement.

KEY OUTPUTS

School systems often use communication audits to

- Strengthen understanding and build support;
- Document program achievements and the value generated by communication investments;
- Set standards for future performance, inspiring the vision needed to support school success; and
- Build the involvement, credibility, and transparency essential to long-term success.

The audit process generally unfolds over 2 or 3 months. Initially, auditors analyze current communication initiatives by reviewing existing communication research and performing content reviews and analyses of current communication efforts. Armed with these initial analyses, auditors then move on—using surveys, focus groups, and in-depth interviews—to collect insights and information from all key constituencies in the school system, both internal and external. One of the goals is to identify strengths and weaknesses by directly engaging representatives from a broad cross section of a school system's key internal and external audiences.

Internally, auditors might seek to promote involvement in the process by central office staff, board members or trustees, building principals and program directors, assistant principals and other supervisors, non-teaching professional staff (psychologists, counselors, curriculum specialists, and so on), teachers, and all support staff.

Externally, auditors might seek to promote involvement by parents (broken down by involved and uninvolved, elementary and high school, special programs, and so on), students, alumni, volunteers, taxpayers (including those with no children in schools), senior citizens, school neighbors, vendors, business leaders, civic group leaders, faith and community leaders, elected officials, news media representatives, and other groups relevant to a school system's particular needs.

The auditing process culminates in a written assessment of current communication efforts—reporting both facts and perceptions, and offering recommendations for improving communication and involvement of the various publics of the schools. In addition, it provides a framework for ongoing involvement as the findings of the audit are shared and used to refine, revise, and initiate communication activities.

WHEN TO AUDIT

For Karen H. Kleinz, veteran school public relations executive and communication auditor, the communication audit process can be used to serve districts with comprehensive communication programs as well as school systems just beginning to formalize their communication programs. Kleinz, associate director of NSPRA, has 29 years of experience in public relations. She directs NSPRA's public engagement, including collaborative partnerships with the Annenberg Institute for School Reform, the Study Circles Resource Center, and the Kettering Foundation. Kleinz also coordinates NSPRA's communication audit service for school districts. She serves as lead auditor on numerous communication audits annually, in addition to serving as contributing auditor on all audits conducted by NSPRA.

When asked why school systems should consider the communication audit process, Kleinz noted (in written responses to submitted questions),

> Whether a district has a long-established communication office, has just recently implemented or is in the process of creating a formal program, or simply recognizes communication is important but lacks the capacity to have a position dedicated to PR/communications, it is key to the success of the communication effort to understand how communication flows across the district—both internally and externally.
>
> Taking a shotgun approach to communication—load up your messages and fire at random, hoping you connect with someone—simply isn't effective in today's tech-savvy communication world. In order to communicate effectively and in a cost-efficient manner, districts must understand where stakeholders are getting their information, what information they want to receive that they may not be getting now, and what the favored vehicles are for delivering information.
>
> They also need to know what current perceptions are held about the school system and what issues stakeholders consider to be most important when it comes to the schools in their community. Conducting a communication audit provides the baseline research needed to build a truly effective communication program that reaches audiences with messages that resonate and build a climate of trust and accountability in the community and with staff.

Supplementing What Exists

Kleinz observed that the research aspect of a communication audit can be helpful in supplementing other research efforts—or it can help to set the stage for new outreach and research initiatives. She explained,

> An audit can be used either way. As a precursor to a comprehensive community survey, it can help to surface issues and concerns that the survey can then pursue with a wider constituency. Or, the audit can take key findings from a research survey or project and probe into them in more detail with focus groups to get a better sense of the values driving a particular issue.

The process of engaging with stakeholders gets under way as soon as the communication audit process begins. Kleinz noted,

> In almost every district we have conducted audits in, we have heard from focus-group participants that it's the first time they have actually been asked to give their opinion or participate in such a process. And when asked how the district can improve communication in the future, they often say "continue to hold meetings (focus groups) like this." I think when used in a planned and purposeful manner, this type of process is very effective at engaging people in a meaningful way.
>
> Another one of the positive aspects of a communication audit is that it asks stakeholders to share their points of view on what is working or not in communication. We often hear from participants in the process that it's the first time they've ever been asked their opinion on anything the district is doing. A communication audit is a great way to demonstrate that the district is serious about hearing from constituents and is making a commitment to improving communication.
>
> If the superintendent is new to the system and community, an audit is a powerful way to position the superintendent as a "listening leader" and shift the culture to one that is more communication-centered. It also will provide the superintendent with important information so that he or she can begin [his or her] tenure with a clear understanding of where communication must be improved or enhanced to rebuild or protect the district's reputation.

It is important to encourage internal and external stakeholders to participate and share their opinions and suggestions so that the district can better meet their communication needs. Districts need to be clear about why they are conducting the audit and stress how important it is that they hear from the various identified groups.

MANAGING REACTIONS

School leaders also need to be ready to answer questions and address concerns during the process. Kleinz warned,

> School officials may be questioned on why they are spending money on a communication audit when there are other needs to be addressed in the schools. There may also be skepticism from some if the district has conducted assessments in the past and never reported back on the outcomes. These folks will question the value of conducting another study that the district won't act on. This is why it is imperative that district leaders close the communication loop from start to finish of the audit process.
>
> When discussing the value of the communication audit process, it also is important to point out that all programs should be assessed for effectiveness and to identify where improvements and enhancements can be made. Auditing the communication program is no different than conducting a curriculum audit. It ensures that communications are supporting the mission and goals of the district, meeting the needs of stakeholders, and that the dollars being allocated to communications are being maximized. It makes good fiscal sense to keep the communication program as effective, efficient, and targeted as possible.

CREATING LEGITIMACY

The outside insight provided by the communication audit process often produces surprises for school officials—who might have thought that they were already connected to their community's thinking and priorities. Kleinz explained,

> I think what often surprises district leaders is that they are often off target on what they think they know about stakeholder perceptions, particularly those of external groups. Because the

audit process engages a broader group of representative voices than those districts generally interact with—PTA/PTO leaders, special-interest groups that regularly attend board meetings, select community leaders, teacher union leaders, and so on— they may hear a very different perspective on issues and concerns held by the broader populace.

They also often discover that the communication vehicles that have become institutionalized—quarterly print newsletters, for example—are seen as irrelevant and unnecessary. Other surprises and frustrations they have are hearing that their communication efforts aren't hitting the mark and people aren't hearing the message they thought they were sending or that the message is not perceived as credible.

I think there are a couple of things that make communication audits particularly effective. [First,] NSPRA relies on only experienced auditors who know how to facilitate the focus groups in a way that allows them to listen objectively and probe into the perceptions of participants without unduly driving answers in a particular direction. They are also skilled at creating a welcoming climate that allows participants to feel comfortable and safe in sharing their honest opinions. Second, I think that the process runs more smoothly when outside auditors are used.

While it is possible for a district to conduct its own audit process, it is difficult to gain the trust of participants that their input is being gathered and processed in a completely unbiased manner. Participants are also hesitant to be as open with the answers when talking to district administrators. This is why we do not allow any district employees or board members to observe the focus groups we conduct.

STUDENT SUCCESS

Communication efforts directly support both district strategies and student achievement—so audits designed to support communications also support district and student needs, Kleinz emphasized. She explained,

The audit process provides a framework for building a comprehensive communication plan that focuses on supporting the strategic plan goals and the overall mission of the district.

When communication efforts are planned and strategic, they play an integral role in supporting student achievement and demonstrating accountability to the community. And, they are also more cost-effective when incorporated into the overall strategic plan.

Sharing the findings of the communication audit with the entire community is an important part of an audit's engagement process. Kleinz suggested,

Sharing the findings of the communication audit with the entire community is an important part of an audit's engagement process. . . . "The results should be shared, warts and all, if the district truly wants to improve communication."

It's absolutely imperative that the district be open and transparent in sharing the final audit report. If, like so many other studies we hear about in school districts, it's looked at by administrators and the board but those who shared their input never hear about it again, then the whole purpose of conducting the communication audit is for naught. The results should be shared, warts and all, if the district truly wants to improve communication.

The communication audit report is, in essence, the foundation research that the district can now use to demonstrate that it "listened" and [that it can now work toward] progress and improvement in strengthening the communication program. I recommend that focus-group participants receive a complete copy of the final report to demonstrate good faith that the district is not trying to hide negative input, and to provide participants with something they can use as a reference to hold district leaders accountable for making demonstrable efforts to change and improve communication.

We have found that not only are focus-group participants interested in seeing how their input was used, [but that] others in the community who are aware of the process are as well. Inevitably, at the conclusion of a focus group, participants will ask when the report will be ready and if they can get a copy. I have also been at meetings where the final report was presented and focus-group participants, who were critical of the district with their comments, thanked the board for conducting the audit, asking for constituents' opinions, and making the report available for everyone to see.

It may not always be necessary to share the complete report with all stakeholders—although this is easy to do now by posting it to the district Web site. But at a minimum, the district should offer a summary overview of the key findings and recommendations to anyone interested.

We recommend that the recommendations in the report be used as the framework for a communication plan, and that the district provide regular updates on progress toward communication goals.

THE DUAL ROLE

Veteran school communication auditor and school PR expert Susan Hardy Brooks agrees that communication audits can serve a dual role of boosting involvement while improving communication efforts. Hardy Brooks has counseled executives on a range of leadership, strategic planning, marketing, and communications issues for more than 28 years. Since starting her Oklahoma-based company in 1998, she has provided strategic counsel to more than 50 clients in the private, public, and nonprofit sectors. Hardy Brooks Public Relations (HBPR) provides strategic counsel to organizations on communications, public relations, marketing, and management issues. HBPR has worked with a range of private companies, nonprofit organizations, schools, and education-related agencies and associations, and specializes in strategic planning, branding, process improvement, and market research.

Hardy Brooks, who has conducted communication audits for NSPRA since 1994, said the process offers universal appeal. She explained,

Any school system can benefit from conducting a communication audit. The real issue is timing. It is important to consider the time of year, the system's internal culture, and any external issues beyond the system's control that might significantly alter the results. The results of the audit research might be different, for instance, if an audit is conducted on the heels of a contentious boundary change issue or an internal breakdown in salary negotiations.

It is best to conduct a communication audit during the actual school year and at a time when there aren't many hot issues or controversies. Communication audits are especially helpful when there is a change in leadership at the superintendent level or director-of-communications level, or when the system is beginning a strategic planning process. It is also important to have buy-in and support from a majority of the board members or trustees.

A communication audit provides a snapshot of how people inside and outside the school system feel about the schools' reputations, leadership, progress, and plans for the future. An audit will often bring issues or problems to the surface that will improve the system's reputation and effectiveness if they are properly resolved. The audit also provides recommendations for addressing major communications issues. In addition to addressing major systemic issues, some issues may surface that are specific to a particular group, such as elementary school parents or business leaders. In these instances, there may be some smaller quick actions the school leaders could take to get big results.

STAGES OF EFFECTIVENESS

Hardy Brooks has seen how the auditing process also can be used by school systems to plan or assess efforts and how the process offers value regardless of the history of communication research or community involvement within a school system. She explained,

A communication audit is effective at several stages in a school system's overall communication research efforts. In some cases, schools have conducted telephone or online surveys prior to a communication audit, then used the results to guide development of the questions for audit focus-group sessions. In other cases, the audit has come early in the research process, with follow-up quantitative surveys to confirm and expand the research results.

A school system may conduct an audit as preliminary research before developing a strategic plan, or wait and conduct an audit to measure progress on the plan a year or two into implementation. The most important thing is to use a blend of quantitative, qualitative, and secondary research on an ongoing basis to shape the system's communications and strategic priorities. Some types of research can be conducted annually, such as phone surveys, to measure the system's reputation and develop benchmarks for progress. Other types of research, such as quick online surveys, can be highly targeted and conducted throughout the year. Communication audits should be conducted on a 3- to 5-year timeline because they require more time and resources.

ONGOING INVOLVEMENT

Success, however, depends on engaging key audiences throughout the auditing process, according to Hardy Brooks.

> The success of a communication audit is highly dependent on the communication that occurs before, during, and after the process. The reasons for the audit should be clearly communicated to everyone. Reasons might include improved communication and customer service, efforts to improve student achievement, overall quality improvement, strategic plan development, the importance of community conversations and dialogue in shaping the school's future, and so on.
>
> Audiences need to know that their input is important and vital to the future of the schools, students, and the community, and that the school system wants to know what they think. Their role is to spend about an hour discussing their thoughts and ideas with a group of their peers. They need to know the number of focus groups being conducted and about how many people will participate in their session.
>
> On a technical level, audiences need to be invited to participate, and then they need to receive a follow-up call confirming their attendance and a reminder call the day before their focus groups are scheduled to meet. Traditional, voice, and e-mail messages should be used to assure that information gets through to participants.
>
> In the focus-group sessions, participants need to know that their comments will remain anonymous and confidential, how their input will be included in the audit report, whether or not they will receive the results, and what the board, trustees, and school leaders plan to do with the results.

BUILDING CREDIBILITY

The audit process itself can be used to build credibility for the school system and its leaders, Hardy Brooks said. She noted,

Internal audiences are usually the most skeptical and raise questions about the confidentiality of their responses and sometimes fear retribution if they are totally honest. They need to be assured by school leaders and outside auditors that their information will not negatively impact them personally, but will become part of an overall big-picture view of trends and issues in the system.

Internal and external audiences always want assurance that something will actually be done with the audit results and recommendations. Audiences often say they have been asked their opinions many times and that nothing has changed as a result. The cynicism is sometimes due to inaction on previous research efforts, but most often it is due to the fact that the communication loop was not closed and audiences simply didn't receive follow-up information spelling out how their input contributed to particular outcomes or actions.

Communication audits provide a great tool for engaging audiences because they don't require a commitment from the audiences to multiple meetings or discussions. They can also provide a springboard for continued dialogue because participants appreciate the opportunity to share their ideas and opinions and listen to other participants' perspectives.

Frequently, focus-group participants will say that the school system should continue to have conversations like the focus-group sessions. The focus-group process is invaluable because it gets people talking about the schools and most often creates a lot of goodwill among participants. A school system that is considering an ongoing community-engagement initiative would benefit from the communication audit experience.

DIVIDENDS OF TRANSPARENCY

While getting an audit under way will present obstacles and perhaps even spark some controversy, Hardy Brooks noted that keeping the process transparent and involving everyone in the process is the best antidote to any skepticism. And, she emphasized, the positive outcomes from the process are well worth the effort. She explained,

Once school leaders have approved the expenditure for conducting a communication audit, the logistics of setting up the focus groups are probably the most difficult part of the process.

Scheduling rooms, [arranging] consecutive focus-group sessions, and securing participants is challenging for school staff. Once the auditors make their site visit and the focus groups are under way, school staff members have the hardest part of the work behind them.

Probably the most surprising outcome during the audit process is the overwhelmingly positive and instant response school leaders receive from focus-group participants, who come out of the sessions feeling good about the process and the opportunity to be a part of the discussion.

For school systems with well-managed and strategic communications already in place, an audit often confirms and expands on the effective work being done not only in the communications department, but at all levels throughout the school system. Sometimes positive internal benchmarks or best practices are identified, which need to be integrated system-wide. Other times, inconsistencies in communication across departments and schools are identified, and processes are recommended to assure consistent communication.

In school systems where communication has not been a priority in the past, the audit process immediately catapults communications to the top of the list because for a few days and weeks everyone is talking and thinking about its importance and value to the system. The audit recommendations can often provide the central elements of a school system's strategic communications plan, or can help systems identify things they don't need to be doing anymore [with regard to] communication.

Regardless of the sophistication of the communications efforts, the audit recommendations help school systems get a better return on their communications investment, help internal audiences recognize their roles and responsibilities in communication, and involve the community in taking ownership of the schools and making schools better.

Transparency remains vital as the auditing process concludes and results are communicated. Community involvement needs to continue as audit findings are reviewed and discussed.

Transparency remains vital as the auditing process concludes and results are communicated. Community involvement needs to continue as audit findings are reviewed and discussed, Hardy Brooks explained. She noted,

Transparency is the key to effectively reporting audit findings. At the very least, every participant in a focus group should receive a copy of the executive summary of the audit. It would be even better to share the entire report with them, along with a reminder that their involvement helped shape the results and a game plan for moving forward with the recommendations.

A complete audit report should also be shared with the board, trustees, and leadership teams. In leadership team meetings, a discussion of key elements and recommendations should be discussed, and key messages should be developed for sharing the information with staff and constituents.

Timing of distribution should have the report going to focus-group participants and staff immediately following the board presentation and discussion.

Some school systems post the audit in its entirety on their Web sites as well, for the entire community to view.

To carry "closing the communications loop" to the next level, it would be great if participants, staff, and school leaders received progress reports on implementation of the recommendations included in the audit on a quarterly or annual basis, or through real-time postings on the Web site.

VALUE

Now and Later

Both short- and long-term involvement and communication are enhanced following a communication audit. Hardy Brooks said,

> The biggest direct benefit of conducting a communication audit is creating a better return on the school system's communications investment. School systems are able to identify what is and is not working in their efforts to communicate with all audiences, and can disinvest in some efforts and increase investment in others.
>
> An audit helps educators and the community recognize the critical link between communication and achievement of the system's strategic goals. By looking at communication systemically, the audit provides school systems with ideas for process improvement, which are often difficult for internal staff to see.

Schools are able to find out what their reputation is among internal and external groups, and work to address any weaknesses or challenges that are identified. Internal groups and school leaders recognize their role in effective communication and how it impacts student achievement and the system's overall effectiveness.

In the short term, a communication audit brings a laser-like focus on a school system's communication efforts for a few days or weeks. Internal and external audiences become more aware of what, how, and why the district communicates and its impact. Focus-group participants feel more connected to the school system in the short term, and generally feel optimistic about the system's future and how they can contribute to it. The goodwill created by the audit process will quickly fade, however, if there is a lack of follow-through and communication of audit results.

In the long term, an audit can help shape and improve a school system's reputation, or brand. It can provide strategic direction for the future in broad, systemic ways, and in communications specifically. An audit can lead to increased community support and better bond election results. It can result in better community and business partnerships, the development of ongoing dialogue about the future of the schools, and better relationships with key opinion leaders, parents, and stakeholders. It can also lead to an increased commitment of financial and staffing resources to communication.

Effective communication is essential to the school system's success in student achievement, strategic direction, community support, customer—that is, student—satisfaction, parental involvement, employee morale, and even a community's economic vitality and quality of life. Administrators who recognize these vital links can begin to create understanding and support with their boards, employees, and communities through participation in the audit process.

THREE COMMUNICATION AUDIT CASES

The following insights come from school administrators who have conducted audits of their school systems, and who were directly involved in the process.

Rochelle Cancienne-Touchard, Director of Public Information

St. Charles Parish Public Schools, Luling, LA

Q. Why did you decide to pursue a communication audit?

A. I decided to recommend that we conduct a communication audit in our district because we were in the infancy of our communications program. The district had just hired a public information officer for external communications and a public information officer for internal communications. The problem was that each position was supervised by a different person. As the PIO [public information officer] for external communications, I reported directly to the superintendent. The PIO for internal communications reported to another staff member. In essence, the right hand did not know what the left hand was doing. The goal of pursuing the audit was to identify the obvious weaknesses, and confirm the areas that were working with the hopes of gaining feedback on how we could improve.

Q. How did this audit fit into your overall communication research activity?

A. The audit was more of an initial research effort to collect data and insights as well as to set benchmarks.

Q. How did you communicate with internal and external audiences before and during the process?

A. I identified key stakeholders within our school system as well as in the community who I felt would provide truthful feedback regarding communication efforts in the district. I made personal phone calls to each focus-group participant and followed up with a formal invitation to participate in the process.

My key message to each person was to encourage them to provide honest answers to the questions that would be asked by the facilitators. Our goal was to improve the way we communicated with stakeholders; this could only be done if honest feedback was provided.

Q. What were the kinds of questions or skepticism you faced from those internal or external audiences?

A. For the most part, they were thankful for being given the opportunity to participate in the process. The question of confidentiality of responses was asked quite often by our employees. I reassured them that no one from the district [high-level administrators] would be sitting in on the focus-group sessions. I guess they were concerned about retaliation for their responses.

Q.   How did you find the communication audit process worked as a way to involve or engage internal and external audiences?

A.   I thought the process was outstanding. The structure allowed me to involve a member from every sector of the community in addition to a cross section of employees. I scheduled 25 focus groups in the two days that the facilitators were here. If you want to get the most bang for your buck, involve those individuals in your focus groups who might not be your biggest fans but are your biggest critics. This gives them an opportunity to be a part of the solution.

Q.   What was the most difficult aspect of the communication audit process for you and your staff?

A.   I think the most difficult part of the process was setting up the times for the focus groups in a two-day period while trying to accommodate everyone's schedule.

Q.   What outcomes or recommendations from the audit were most beneficial to your system and its communication efforts?

A.   Every recommendation from the audit was beneficial. The most immediate change was to redesign the department so that it actually functioned as a department. This set the tone to start implementing change. Some of those changes, to name just a few, included

- Development of a Comprehensive Communications Plan;
- Expanding opportunities for parent–community communication and involvement;
- Expansion and improvement of school newsletters; and
- Upgrades/revisions to our Web site.

Q.   How did you share the results of your audit with those who participated?

A.   Our findings were presented at a public school board meeting. I invited all those who participated to be a part of the audience when the findings were presented. This allowed everyone to see that the feedback given truly played a role in the final recommendations. People were genuinely interested in the results because this was the first time a communication audit had been conducted in the district.

Q. How would you characterize the value of conducting a communication audit?

A. I can't even begin to explain the impact that this audit had on our district. As I mentioned before, there was no semblance of a communication program in place 1-year prior to the audit. The district had hired two professionals to carry out its communication efforts but failed to put a structure in place that would facilitate the process. The recommendations from the audit validated the need to redesign the Public Information Department in order to increase effectiveness. This, in addition to many other recommendations, put us in a position to truly implement effective changes in how and what we used to communicate to stakeholders. It is still paying off 9 years later.

Q. What advice or suggestions would you offer to other school administrators considering the communication audit process for their school systems?

A. If you have never had a communication audit conducted in your school system, now is the time. It will be the best money you ever spend. The audit results can be one of the most valuable tools to use to improve the communication efforts in your district. I especially recommend the audit to those public relations professionals who have new superintendents in their districts. What a powerful message to send to employees, students, parents, and community members that "we are interested in what you have to say to help us better communicate with you."

The audit results can be one of the most valuable tools to use to improve the communication efforts in your district. I especially recommend the audit to those public relations professionals who have new superintendents in their districts.

Paul Tandy, Director of Public Affairs

Parkway School District, St. Louis, MO

Q. Why did you decide to pursue a communication audit?

A. We hadn't conducted an external audit of our communications program in more than 15 years. During that time, we had experienced tremendous changes in terms of how we communicated with our constituents. It seemed as if we continued to add programs and activities, but never thoroughly analyzed others that might need to be changed or removed. In discussing the issues with the members of my volunteer public relations advisory committee, we decided to pursue an external audit by a professional communications firm. Initially the response was not well received by the superintendent due to costs. However, I was able to leverage the volunteer PR professionals on the committee to help convince the superintendent and school board to move forward and treat it as an important investment.

Q. How did this audit fit into your overall communication research activity?

A. We conduct a random community opinion survey every 2 years to track overall opinions of the district, including our communications program. This audit was intended to provide more qualitative data to complement some of the quantitative data we already had.

Q. How did you communicate with internal and external audiences before and during the process?

A. We hit the messages pretty hard with parents and staff to let them know we wanted their opinions. We told them that their feedback would help shape the overall communications program in the future and that their comments would be anonymous.

Q. What were the kinds of questions or skepticism you faced from those internal or external audiences?

A. One of our focus-group participants attended more than one session on the same topic. She told me later it was because she was skeptical that each meeting would be handled in the same way regardless of who the participants were. She said she realized that she was wrong and that we were genuinely seeking the same input from all audiences.

Q. How did you find the communication audit process worked as a way to involve or engage internal and external audiences?

A. I think it's an effective research and planning tool, but not as much for broad-based public engagement. You can use the data gathered as a starting point for your engagement efforts.

Q. What was the most difficult aspect of the communication audit process for you and your staff?

A. The most difficult step was organizing the focus groups and getting the right people to attend in the right numbers. I think we conducted approximately 15 focus-group sessions with a broad cross section of the community. It's difficult to get people to attend who aren't connected with the schools. That was quite a labor-intensive effort.

Q. What outcomes or recommendations from the audit were most beneficial to your system and its communication efforts?

A. It helped me reorganize my department and prioritize our daily work. I was also able to eliminate one of our employee newsletters right away without any negative feedback. Some of the other recommendations served to validate what we already knew, but we had needed an "expert" to reinforce the message with the district leadership so we could act on it with confidence. There were a few surprises such as the recommendation to re-initiate our key communicator program, which we thought the community didn't support.

Q. How did you share the results of your audit with those who participated?

A. We provided written summaries to all focus-group participants, along with a copy of the final report. We invited them back to a few meetings to discuss the results. We presented the report at a public school board meeting and issued a news release, which garnered some positive press. We also discussed the results at the school board's annual planning retreat the following summer. This helped board members make a change to one of the district's areas of strategic focus.

Q. How would you characterize the value of conducting a communication audit?

A. I wouldn't do it very often, but it is an invaluable tool for getting a deep level of feedback on existing programs. It provides enough detail and clarity that you can really act to make changes with confidence.

Q. What advice or suggestions would you offer to other school administrators considering the communication audit process for their school systems?

A. All districts should do it, particularly if they're experiencing a lot of change, such as enrollment shifts, demographic changes, or financial changes. . . . You should also perform an audit if you don't already have some sort of mechanism to gather input for your program—regardless of the level of changes you're experiencing.

For us, it really didn't affect the district's overall strategic decision making or goal setting. However, for my department and our planning, it was extremely valuable from a tactical and operational standpoint.

Kim Cranston, Chief Communications Officer

Rockwood School District, Wildwood, MO

Q. Why did you decide to pursue a communication audit?

A. We were in the process of revising our comprehensive communications plan. Rockwood had never conducted a communication audit. We wanted an outside, objective review of our communications efforts so we could look at ways to improve them.

Q. How did this audit fit into your overall communication research activity?

A. It was more of an initial research effort to collect data and insights and set some new benchmarks.

Q. How did you communicate with internal and external audiences before and during the process?

A. We shared information with our key communicator groups, both internal and external. Here is a summary of what we shared:

One of the tenets of the Rockwood School District is data-driven decision making. The importance of this process is reflected in every function of our organization.

In terms of communication, research and data are critical. It is essential to know how our different audiences prefer to receive information, what information they want and need, and how we can improve the effectiveness of our communication with them.

In the spirit of continuous improvement, we have contracted with the National School Public Relations Association (NSPRA) to conduct a district-wide communication audit. The purposes of the audit are [to]

- Take a snapshot of current internal and external communication activities;
- Discover what's working and what's not working;
- Learn best ways to communicate with key target audiences;
- Assess content, channels, and frequency [that best meet the] needs of audiences;
- Assess communication capacity and credibility of communications efforts;
- Provide baseline data to measure progress in the future.

The process will involve NSPRA's review of existing communication policies, publications, and strategies. Their auditors will conduct a number of focus groups, composed of people who represent our various internal and external audiences, in order to hear what they have to say about district and school communication.

They will prepare an audit report of their key findings, observations, and recommendations based on their analysis of current communication activities and information gleaned from the focus groups.

NSPRA conducts audits for school districts across the country. Districts such as Forsyth County in Georgia, Jefferson County in Colorado, and Tempe School District in Arizona that have been recognized for their outstanding communication efforts have utilized an NSPRA audit.

Q. What were the kinds of questions or skepticism you faced from those internal or external audiences?

A. We really didn't have any—the only people who expressed any skepticism were a couple of our board members. We focused on a commitment to continuous improvement and the need to operate from "what we *know* we know" as opposed to "what we *think* we know."

Q. How did you find the communication audit process worked as a way to involve or engage internal and external audiences?

A. The audit worked well in terms of engaging stakeholders because all stakeholder groups had an opportunity to participate—this was especially important for our staff.

Q. What was the most difficult aspect of the communication audit process for you and your staff?

A. The most difficult part was organizing and arranging the focus groups. It was a challenge to get these set up. The district calendar was already set for the year, and there were limited times available.

Q. How did you share the results of your audit with those who participated?

A. We shared the results with the Board and everyone who participated in the process. Additionally, we posted the report on our district Web site so anyone could review the audit findings.

Q. What advice or suggestions would you offer to other school administrators considering the communication audit process for their school systems?

A. Do it!

Q. What other thoughts, comments, or suggestions would you like to share?

A. For us, the audit provided confirmation that we are on the right track with our plan. It was validating. The audit also provided recommendations that we could easily incorporate into our overall communication plan.

I strongly encourage school districts at all levels or points on the communications planning spectrum to consider an audit. It will

- Give you a fresh, objective view of your current plans and work;
- Provide data for you to use in making decisions;
- Give you specific recommendations for ways to improve; and
- Demonstrate a commitment to continuous improvement.

Audits are a commonly accepted business practice. Our finance and technology departments are audited on a regular basis. Why wouldn't a communications department want the same type of review? It demonstrates a professional approach to this important function of a district or organization.

CONCLUSION

Clearly, communication audits offer school systems direct access to two qualities now in demand: accountability and transparency. But these are just the first two benefits accruing to those who invest in this basic communication research. This relatively inexpensive and straightforward process also can play a key role in engaging all of a district's communities, both internally and externally, with the system and its vision.

Of equal importance, the active involvement that an audit creates supports both student and school achievement. Schools and students simply try harder—and expect more from themselves—when they know that others are involved and that others care about the achievement.

Audits are research, to be sure, but they aspire to be more than basic research efforts. The process is one that collects more than insights and data. Communication auditing involves the entire community in the research and planning activities for communication—modeling the high standard for openness and involvement that communication seeks for the school system overall. During this process, a communication audit builds partners—even supporters—for the entire school system and for existing and resulting communication initiatives.

Communication auditing involves the entire community in the research and planning activities for communication—modeling the high standard for openness and involvement that communication seeks for the school system overall.

Those who use a communication audit can expect it to

- Provide a clear, current analysis of current communication programming and priorities within a time- and cost-effective framework;
- Document what's working—and not working—in communication programming and informational programs;

- Identify key needs so that district leaders can make the best communication choices among those that are available and affordable;
- Suggest message and campaign strategies to make sure that issues are addressed in communication and to align communication tactics with the district's strategic plans and vision;
- Develop audience- and issue-specific recommendations assuring that communication programming fully serves a district's diverse audiences and needs;
- Set benchmarks for future communication performance standards;
- Assure that the system is getting the most from new and emerging communication media, aligning current and potential new-media efforts with the best practices identified in other school systems;
- Actively seek constituent feedback through a community-wide, insight-gathering process that heightens engagement and involvement and sets the foundation for support for school communication efforts going forward.

The National School Public Relations Association has additional information and publications on school communication audits, and its staff can offer advice on audits for local school systems. NSPRA, based in Rockville, Maryland, can be reached at www.nspra.org or 301–519–0496.

REFERENCES

Bagin, D., Gallagher, D. R., & Moore, E. H. (2008). *The school and community relations* (9th ed.). Boston: Pearson/Allyn & Bacon.

Grunig, J. E., & Hunt, T. (1984). *Managing public relations.* Orlando, FL: Holt, Rinehart and Winston.

Moore, E. H. (2008). *School PR research primer: Practical ideas for getting data, driving decisions, and empowering programs.* Rockville, MD: National School Public Relations Association.

National School Public Relations Association. (2002). *Raising the bar for school PR: New standards for the school public relations profession.* Retrieved March 1, 2010, from http://www.nspra.org/files/docs/ StandardsBooklet.pdf.

Wilcox, D., Ault, P., Agee, W., & Cameron, G. (2000). *Public relations strategies and tactics* (6th ed.). New York: Longman.

CHAPTER SEVEN

MANAGE THE MOLEHILL BEFORE IT BECOMES A MOUNTAIN

Keeping Parent Interactions Productive for Students

LIN KUZMICH

THE INITIAL INTERACTION WITH AN ANGRY PARENT

Your secretary has just informed you that a parent wants to see you *right now*—and that parent is steaming mad. After sighing loudly, you instruct the secretary to bring the parent into your office. You mentally brace yourself for the anger. Your communication in the next few moments is critical.

Parents react negatively to school events and interactions from three basic perspectives.

1. Parents love their children and want the best for them, so parents act on behalf of those they love.

2. Parents act based on personal past experiences that may not be positive, so parents act to prevent unfair treatment from happening to their children.

3. Parents respond to school events with an overflow of emotions from the world, so a school event can be an opportunity to vent stress or frustration that originates from other sources.

Leaders need to learn that in the first few seconds of interaction with a parent, none of these matters. For a clearly angry parent, only a few responses will work, and the leader does not have much time.

These situations occur every day and at every level in our schools. Dealing with angry parents, staff members, students, and community members is an unavoidable part of our duties. The key for administrators is to have a set of effective communication tools ready to deploy. We must address, in a safe and supportive environment, the real emotions that surround the education of young people. The tools that follow include de-escalation methods, listening strategies, methods for getting closure in tough situations, and prevention methods.

Dealing with angry parents, staff members, students, and community members is an unavoidable part of our duties. The key for administrators is to have a set of effective communication tools ready to deploy.

DE-ESCALATION STRATEGIES

There are three de-escalation strategies that work most of the time. First is *the social positive,* which requires the leader to personally greet the parent at the door with an outstretched hand, ready to shake and say, "I am really glad you decided to come to school today and visit about [insert student's name]. Come on in. Can I get you a cold soda or some coffee?" The parent will react either by telling you that you won't be so glad he or she came (retaining the anger), or the parent will respond to the social situation and the offered beverage. If he or she responds to the beverage choice, then you have a chance to further de-escalate, as the parent is appreciating your initial respect. If the parent remains angry, take a seat, get out a pad of paper, and say, "Tell me about it."

A second move—*the neutral territory* approach—is to have the parent taken to a neutral conference room and offered a beverage by the secretary, who tells the parent that you are completing a meeting or phone call and will be in shortly. This is important for two reasons: First, it gets the angry parent out of the hall or front office, and second, it gives you time to look up the incident or speak briefly with the staff member involved. It also allows you to note the parent's response to waiting. Does the parent call someone and start screaming about the school, does the person pace, or does he or she sit quietly? For some parents, this approach allows enough of a pause between the hassle of getting to the school and then getting your attention in the waiting area that they calm down just a bit. Sometimes, however, a few minutes of waiting only escalates their anger. Either way, do not keep the parent waiting very long. Do not use the second method for parents who come with someone else, since the interaction of two or more people will continue to maintain the anger level.

The third method of greeting is *the commitment.* This method is used when you need time or the parent must wait. Come out and personally greet the parent using the first method and bring the individual somewhere inside the office away from students and public spaces. Tell the parent you are going to take just a few minutes (or a certain number of minutes) to clear your schedule so you can really listen to what the parent has to say. Explain that you know he or she is concerned and that you want to provide an opportunity for uninterrupted conversation. Immediately move out of the setting and make certain a secretary or someone takes care of the parent's comfort—hanging up a coat, getting a beverage or snack. Most parents recognize respect when they hear it; your commitment to listen is like gold to an angry parent. Keep your word on the amount of time you're gone, and then be prepared to do just that: listen.

These three methods—the social positive, the neutral territory, and the commitment—work well with 80–90 percent of parents and make the conversation that follows much easier. Initial de-escalation has high payoff for more productive parent interactions and outcomes for students.

Once the initial greeting and attempts at de-escalation are complete, it is time to listen to the parent. Since the parent is still angry, or at least filled with powerful emotions, some listening methods work better than others. (Many of these tools and methods also work very well with highly charged situations involving staff, students, and community members.) Administrators who coach each other on communication strategies will find this chapter helpful for professional advice or supervision. Share these strategies with others as you mentor, coach, or supervise. Most of us would have loved to have known these methods early in our careers as leaders.

Tips for Listening to the Angry Parent's Story

Hear a Parent Out and Don't Interrupt

Take notes and jot down your questions. Parents need to tell things their way; if you ask questions too soon, it is often perceived as disrespectful. When a parent starts to wind down, wait to make certain he or she is finished. Usually, a parent will end with a question like, "What are you going to do about this?"

At that point, first go back in your notes and seek clarity. Ask questions about the story without making judgments, offering solutions or reasons, or defending anything. If you try to defend or state rules now, it risks showing disrespect for the entire listening process you just went through. Listen, then clarify, then ask questions. You may not need to make any statements during this conversation. You may simply need to thank the parent and tell him or her that you will take time to look into the situation and get back with them, setting a date and time for the next interaction (which should be as soon as possible).

Some parents are nonsequential in the telling of their story, and you will need to establish an accurate timeline through your follow-up questions. A few parents focus on feelings, some on events, and others on equitable solutions. Keep prompting the parent for the full story before you start questioning or seeking clarity.

Don't Bring in the Child or Staff Member
Involved During the Initial Phases of the Meeting

Even after you listen to the story, wait to investigate before you bring others into the room. The parent might still be angry, and neither the child nor the staff member needs to deal with that anger right now. You will know it's safe to bring others in if the parent is responsive when you indicate that both you and the parent probably have only part of the story, and the rest of the information needs to come from others who were there. If the parent agrees that there is more to the story, you can certainly bring in the child. You may still want to investigate before hosting and mentoring a meeting with the involved staff member or other witnesses.

Never bring someone else's child into the room. That is part of your investigation—not a prerogative of the first parent. You must protect the rights of *everyone's* children.

Buy Time. A Little Time Is Your Friend

Once the parent tells the story and is anxious for you to be on his or her side or to solve the problem, you need time. All that is needed at this point is to say, "Thank you. I will look into it and get back to you by such and such a time."

At this point, the following guidelines must be followed. First, you need to follow due process in any discipline or policy violation incident. Second, the parent should *never* be on the investigation team. Third, if the incident should become a legal issue, the investigation must follow prescribed steps, perhaps including double-checking with your boss and the involvement of law enforcement. Unless you were involved in the incident, have already investigated, or have the police report sitting in front of you, take some time to figure things out.

Do Not Tolerate Ongoing Verbal Abuse or Physical Threats

Try one or two tactics like asking the parent to stop using abusive language or leaving him or her alone for a few minutes while you bring in a beverage or snack. Give the parent time to gain some control. If none of these strategies works, end the meeting. Tell the parent you will be in touch at a later time when you can have a productive conversation that is free of abuse.

In extreme cases, if the parent refuses to leave or creates a public disturbance that may risk harming students, call the police. If the parent comes in abusive and responds to de-escalation, that's great. However, if nothing works, no one should have to endure ongoing abuse for any reason, and you have the right to send that message.

Some parents end a meeting by telling you they will go to your boss. If so, simply give them the contact information for your boss' office—*not* his or her cell phone number. Immediately after the parent leaves, call your boss and let him or her know of the situation and how you are handling it.

In very rare cases, a parent makes a threat of physical harm. Take all such threats against employees or students seriously. Put the school

Your job is to protect the students and staff on your campus, and it is right to protect yourself as well.

in lockdown; get help; and, where necessary, see that a no-trespassing or a restraining order is issued. Your job is to protect the students and staff on your campus, and it is right to protect yourself as well.

Once, a parent threatened our staff, saying she would come back with a weapon and deal with the teacher and me in her own way. The police arrived with impressive speed and helped secure the neighborhood as well. That parent was never allowed on campus again, and the courts dealt with her aggressively since she had prior weapon-related charges on her record.

When such actions are necessary, any administrator's first concern is the safety of the child. Consequently, it is wise to take all the action needed to keep students and staff safe. However, the "police card" is one to play only in extreme circumstances. If security officers are routinely stationed at your school, make use of them where appropriate but do not include them in every parent meeting. You will develop a reputation of disrespect for parents, or fear of parents, and that is counterproductive.

Always Let the Angry Parent
Unload on You—Not on the Staff

It is critical to let your staff be aware that this is your practice. With such an assurance, staff members can cut off an abusive or very angry parent and get help right away. Do not have the staff member sit in when you are called to the classroom or the athletic field. Take the parent to your office or conference room and hear the person out.

There is a big difference between an angry parent and one who is concerned or irritated by a situation. Teach your staff to know the difference. Moreover, teach your staff listening and processing strategies like the ones in this chapter to enable them to handle irritated parents. Too often, we fail to teach our professional and support staff what to do with tougher parents well in advance of the first confrontation. In this highly charged and change-prone era, parents *will* get upset. So plan accordingly. Meet with your staff about ways of dealing with degrees of anger or irritation. We lose too many new teachers because they dread volatile interactions with parents. We can prevent this loss with some well-chosen role plays and a few key strategies, comments, and questions.

Wherever possible, do hold staff members accountable for the de-escalation of parents' angry responses. Some staff members, in the heat of a confrontation, have a tendency to add fuel to the fire by making judgmental statements or trying to teach the parent to parent differently. This does not work; in fact, it often makes matters worse, creating an even bigger problem. If one of your staff members has acted in this manner, bring him or her into your office privately, tell the staff person what you witnessed or what was reported to you, and inform him or her of the behaviors and wording that you expect. After the person responds, share your expectations for his or her actions in the future very clearly, emphasizing the district or school standards for professional behavior and communication.

Your staff should feel safe at work; no one can thrive in an atmosphere of fear. (Setting clear guidelines for visitors to school buildings is often part of state law.) With clear and agreed-upon procedural expectations, office staff can alert you or the administrator on duty if an angry parent is headed to a classroom. Train office staff to try to hold the parent so that the teacher or appropriate staff member can be located. If there is an issue, it gives the teacher time to alert you or others to engage needed assistance before a confrontational meeting.

Don't Try to Solve Confrontations With Athletes' or Competitors' Parents on the Field, at the Game, or at the Event

Help your coaches and activity sponsors by taking an angry parent off the field or out of the sports or competition venue to chat. (This could also apply to band competitions.) Some parents feed on each other or the crowd; you want to remove them from that situation. Some parents become so heated that even taking them someplace else does not work. For those parents, give them your contact information and set up an appointment to address the parent's concerns, or invite the parent to call and make an appointment. Keep the angry parent with you until he or she regains some degree of control. When the parent is ready, be empathic, saying, "I am sorry this seems unfair" or "I am sorry your child feels unfairly treated; tell me more about it." Then follow the procedure I described earlier: Listen without interrupting, take notes, seek clarity, and ask questions. Or schedule a follow-up appointment.

When dealing with the parent of an athlete or competitor, a range of options usually works better than one set procedure, unless the problem is serious, such as causing bodily harm to another student or a coach. A variety of suggestions—offering opportunities to practice improved skills, a chance to play later in the season, a way to deal with peers or referee/judge calls more effectively—tends to work well. Never offer options that are not possible. If follow-up is needed, tell the parent when you will get back to him or her and leave the door open for another conversation.

Take the time to teach your coaches and assistants ways to avoid alienating parents by not losing their temper, becoming defensive, dismissing the parent, or interrupting. Instead, try some of the methods I have suggested; rehearse them with your staff. Sooner or later, if you coach or sponsor competitive activities, you *will* have to deal with angry parents; it is the rule, not the exception. Provide training ahead of time in dealing with such challenging issues.

When parents form a group to come after a coach or sponsor, get involved early, or see that your athletic director is also involved. Always separate the parents, without the coach present, to hear everyone's story fairly. Mob meetings rarely go well.

If parents insist on being together, pass out paper and pens and ask them to (1) state the problem, (2) state their evidence, and (3) list suggested solutions. Collect the papers before allowing any discussion. Read a couple of randomly selected statements of the problem, then ask for clarity. Separate firsthand evidence from that which is repeated to the parents by other students not directly involved, or that is simply hearsay. Deal only with firsthand evidence. Tell parents you will look into the matter and take their suggested solutions into account. In following up with the problem, show parents how you used some or parts of their suggested solutions. This establishes a great deal of credibility with parents of athletes, musicians, or other competitors and also shows them how to work within the system in a productive, nonpunitive way.

In one instance, a large group of girls' basketball parents came to see me, upset with the coach. Accusations were flying; the shouting started right away. When each parent wrote down his or her point of view, the similarity in the firsthand evidence led to further investigation. Every single parent cited the coach's practice of "cussing out" the students on the team bus as evidence that he was a poor role model. Talking to the driver and the coach confirmed these reports, and the coach was given one chance to apologize and discontinue such behavior. (Eventually, we had to change coaches.) This is not the media-fueled major leagues; instead, learning, role modeling, and teaching are what we should be doing in extracurricular activities. Sometimes parents are right, so keep an open mind at all times.

GETTING CLOSURE WITH PARENTS

If the problem can be solved at the initial meeting, that's fine. However, with most angry parents, a follow-up meeting or phone call is necessary so that you have time to investigate. If you already have the needed information—or if you dealt with the initial discipline, confrontation, or other issue directly with the child—then the last phase of the interaction is to develop solutions and closure.

This is the time when understanding the parent's unique perspective is critical. If the parent's concern comes from love or protection of the child, that is one factor. If it is based on the person's own past negative experiences, however, that's a different matter. And when the world is just a tough place for him or her right now, that calls for yet another type of response.

For some parents, of course, their reaction can arise from a combination of different sources. A parent who dwells on getting their child "off the hook" or seeing that the child receives special treatment should first be approached with a statement of the standard for behavior or action expected. Next, the parent should be told what the child actually did, and then asked what he or she thinks would be the best solution to the problem for everyone involved in similar situations.

This approach will help you with the parent who always wants to rescue his or her child, thinks the child is being held to a different standard, or thinks the problem is someone else's. Asking this parent what he or she wants for the child alone is not the best approach since the answer is known. Explain how the system works and the range of options you have as a leader, and make certain the parent knows you have other, tougher options you could take. Asking the parent if a more extreme consequence would be helpful sometimes makes the actual consequence acceptable. Never offer choice where there is no choice in resolving the issue, especially with legal or more rigidly policy-based local regulations.

Never offer choice where there is no choice in resolving the issue, especially with legal or more rigidly policy-based local regulations.

For the parent who has negative past experiences with school, the person's orientation often revolves around the issue of fairness. Parents will ask you how the others involved are being treated and whether similar consequences are occurring. As a matter of fact, dissimilar consequences may cause the problem in the first place with this type of parent. It is important to describe the rules and the range of consequences.

Parents with negative past experiences will often perceive their child as a victim, because they themselves felt powerless or victimized. One contention that comes up frequently is that "My child did not throw the first punch" or was treated unfairly or picked on. In this era of bullying, it is important to understand how to provide a safe environment for all students. If the parent is correct and the child *is* being picked on, deal with that fact and set up an ongoing communication plan. Don't treat it as a single incident that can be tidily resolved. Set up frequent check-in procedures with the parent; seek to create opportunities for the child to learn skills to manage teasing or bullying and for staff members to offer a safe environment as an ongoing piece of the plan. There are some great publications out on taking the bullying out of schools. Some of the works that come to mind right away are *Cyber Kids, Cyber Bullying, Cyber Balance,* by Barbara Trolley and Constance Hanel (2009); *Safe & Secure Schools,* by Judy Brunner and Dennis Lewis (2009); *How to Stop Bullying and Social Aggression,* by Steve Breakstone, Michael Dreiblatt, and Karen Dreiblatt (2009), and *The Respectful School,* by Stephen Wessler (2003).

If it is about who threw the second punch, talk about the child's options at this point, such as walking away, yelling for help, "pushing away to get away," or self-defense, if no other options exist. (At the elementary level, there are always other options on the school grounds during the day, but that is often not the case at the secondary level, where peers "egg on" fights.)

If you have a clear understanding of the situation and the child did try other options first or had no choice, what is the fair approach? Schools with all-or-nothing approaches to discipline frequently cause a show of temper from this type of parent. If a parent knows that you treat each issue and incident with fairly and equitably, considering all points of view, then once you share what you know, the parent will be more willing to understand the consequences.

If, as a result of his or her own past experiences or perceptions, the parent becomes defensive every time a confrontation occurs at school, you will need to work through to solutions with facts and a range of options or choices. This method will help to prevent further instances and will show the parent that you are responding differently from his or her previous experience.

Schools that simply expel a 6-year-old student for bringing in a pocket knife or throwing a defending punch, because that is what the rules state, *will* have ongoing problems. There are always options and degrees in any solution, unless you are dealing with such felony-level instances as drug buys, knife fights, camera-recorded or witnessed theft or vandalism, and rape or other extremely abusive behaviors. In those extreme cases, law enforcement is involved and the legal system takes over. Short of that, however, listen, investigate, and consider the range of consequences or options. What do you want for the future of this child, and what does the parent want? More often than not, you should be able to find common ground.

Angry parents who are simply stressed out by life and by situations beyond the school's control need time. This type of parent is best dealt with later in the day or at a follow-up meeting where a plan can be developed under calmer circumstances. Getting the parent to name the time and place for such a follow-up meeting often defuses the issue, creating a space for better solution development or understanding. If this type of parent calls with a problem, call back a bit later. You may have more success in the evening after supper when things have settled down somewhat, or possibly the next morning. Have whoever took the parent's call tell the caller when you will get back to him or her. Then stick to that time frame or range of times. When you know a parent is going through a tough time, ask about it; be empathetic. Once the parent's needs are met, you can better focus on the needs of the child.

PREVENTING CONFRONTATIONS WITH PARENTS

Here's a valuable tip: *It is always less work to prevent confrontations with parents than to react to them.* Preventing confrontations may take several forms. Leaders have countless opportunities to set the stage for effective communication—e-mails, registration time, report card pickup, phone call systems, and back-to-school nights are only a few.

Here's a valuable tip: It is always less work to prevent confrontations with parents than to react to them.

At the beginning of every school year, try to communicate your expectations. Speak directly to parents, letting them know there is always more than one side to every story and that you look forward to all calls or visits that seek clarification. When a parent comes into school, and before he or she even gets started, thank the parent for caring enough to visit school or even to call. This establishes a respectful environment.

Explain to parents that school is more like work than home.

There are rules for conduct at work or in public that we don't always observe at home. School is no different; it is a public space, and the rules are created for the good of the many. Emphasizing this distinction helps to avoid issues of how things are done at home versus conduct at school. Acknowledging that a parent has a right to treat such issues as self-defense or teasing differently at home is important. Reminding parents what would happen at work or in the grocery store if the same interaction occurred often comes as a surprise. Establishing school as a public place where different rules apply is very helpful.

Invite parents in to discuss ways in which the school can improve.

As a principal, having parents come for coffee and goodies before or after work; getting feedback; and then publicly acknowledging the helpful suggestions in a newsletter, online, or in other forms of communication help parents see that public opinion matters to you and to the school. This behavior has a very high payoff and can be used as an example of your willingness to listen.

Conducting parent surveys works well, especially when you report the majority point of view. Parents sometimes tell you that "everyone" wants an event, a certain treatment, or a particular response. Conducting an anonymous survey avoids disagreements over holiday-related events at elementary schools, or dances at the middle school level, or eliminating a sport or activity at the high school.

If you set out to accomplish something controversial, and you have some latitude to make choices, collect some parent data first so you can use it with those who might become upset by changes. At one elementary school, we wanted to set up periodic events to allow all students to perform for parents rather than holding a single holiday-based program. At a secondary school, we had to change the high school block schedule to conform to state laws regarding time in school. In both cases, getting parent input through surveys or interviews was helpful. In the case of the high school, just allowing parents to vent was important since the change was required and choice was not an option. Plan to handle controversy rather than allowing controversy to handle you.

Be honest when no choices are available.

If there is a legal issue—for instance, a violation of a policy directive from above—be honest with parents. Do not place blame with others as a regular habit, however; your credibility suffers when you don't take responsibility for your decisions.

When you have no choice on an issue or feel strongly about it, state your decision and the reasoning behind it. Let the parent react and then acknowledge that you must agree to disagree. Leave the opportunity in place for future interaction by remaining cordial even if the parent is not. It is always better if the parent can take a little something away. Even saying that you will note this incident and discuss it with other administrators for future development and refinement of district policy and rules sometimes gives the parent just enough dignity and voice.

Follow the 24-hour rule for communication or callbacks.

Never make parents wait longer than 24 hours to hear from you when they have a concern. This is both respectful and de-escalating. After you figure out what caused the call, addressing it sooner is better. Sometimes allowing an unhappy parent to cool off is a desirable move—just don't wait too long.

Make positive contacts with the home a rule.

Schools that are highly successful with parents keep up a steady flow of communication to the home that is positive and specific to the child. A brief note home or a phone call about what the child learned or did well will make any future issues less arduous.

Some schools follow a "three positive to one negative" contact rule. For larger schools, this might be difficult, but creating some way to ensure regular communication of what goes well is important. For a special-needs student to get a parent signature on an "A" paper rather than an "F" paper is powerful. A call home to a parent about an act of kindness or a great choice sends wonderful messages.

In our office, we had a jar in which we placed the names of students we caught doing great things for others. I picked several of those students' names each week, and we enjoyed a special lunch together. This practice works especially well in the spring, when students get a little antsier and discipline problems tend to spike.

One high school principal I know has staff members call in each parent of a ninth grader at the first parent conference—not to talk about grades but to share their dreams for their son or daughter so that the school can help the child achieve those dreams. Those kinds of practices send priceless messages to parents about our caring, our relationships with students, and our focus on what is good and right for children of any age.

Train your office staff to respond positively to parents and visitors.

First impressions are extremely important. A grouchy receptionist or clerk can do more harm to a school's public relations than any call at a football game or any disciplinary event. How the phone is answered, how long it takes a parent to get to a real person in an automated phone system, and how long before a call is returned are essential procedures to establish for leaders who insist upon proactive communication and follow-through. Proper greeting rituals, treating parents with a welcoming and helpful attitude that shows they belong there, and paying attention to parent comfort such as by getting coffee for visitors or offering an umbrella—all these and more make a school a better place for parents.

In order to accomplish this important goal, training is essential—and one-shot training never works. Meet with your office and support staff each month for better communication. Ask staff members to bring tough issues with parents to these meetings, and work out solutions together as a way of modeling desired behaviors and practices.

When necessary, remove a staff member from the main greeting area if he or she is unable to exhibit desired behaviors. A negative person should never work or even substitute in your main reception area. Take such action before you risk damaging public relations. Substitute teachers are a great source of information about a building's culture. We gave out short questionnaires (just as many restaurants do), and offered candy or a granola bar for filling them out. We used the impressions of substitutes and visitors to make needed changes in our school culture.

Manage the molehill before it becomes a mountain.

This is easier said than done. Often it takes experience to recognize potential mountains in the early stages. Heading off small problems is about knowing your culture, your staff, your students, and your community—and that kind of knowledge takes time to develop.

When I was a central office administrator supervising principals, I noticed that new principals tend to take on issues that are little

Heading off small problems is about knowing your culture, your staff, your students, and your community—and that kind of knowledge takes time to develop.

and make them way too big at first. Sometimes they just need to experience the upheaval so that it can be turned into a teachable moment. Most of the time, however, teaching a little prevention is important.

Look at strategies in terms of people, places, and events. First, learn about the people in your building who tend to "stir the pot" and, many times, agitate more than they contribute solutions. These are the folks who cause "mountains" to form unnecessarily. Dealing with their issues swiftly, and with zero ambiguity, is important. Some staff members need more "air time" with you than others. Be prepared to give that time—within reason, of course—and you can prevent issues from getting too big. Some parents are like that as well. The sooner you get to them, the better—before they call half the neighborhood, your boss, or the media.

Places throughout your service area—athletic events, swimming pools, field trips, lunchrooms, gyms, bathrooms, and many other locales—can be possible sources of problems that can be prevented or dealt with before they become too large. Address safety issues and ongoing discipline before you have to react to more serious incidents.

Some events—football games, assemblies, cheerleading tryouts, turkey dinner in first-grade classes, birthday balloon deliveries, and even cell phone usage—are also predictable as possible sources of problems. Therefore, the more you communicate in advance with your various stakeholders about expectations and consequences, the better. Having a cheerleading coach, for example, who sends home tips on how to handle the situation if a child does not make the team can be enormously helpful. Preparing staff members for the unexpected drills or requirements of testing is another essential example.

If you are not good at logistics or thinking about the details of events, find or hire people on your staff who excel at this; it will save you many headaches and prevent several eruptive, mountainous consequences. After a decade or so in administration, you can tell when you send a student out of your office that a phone call or visit from a parent will result. Learn to call the parent before the student gets home or tells his or her version. This can help in many ways. The parent will realize when the child is giving only part of the story, the phone call back to you (invite parents to call you back with more questions) will be less angry, and solutions will be more possible.

The moral here is this: When you keep small problems small, you actually get time to be an instructional leader, to form relationships with students and staff, and to become the effective leader you wanted to be in the first place.

CONCLUSION

Students form lasting memories and responses to schools not only through their own personal experiences, but also from the reactions of their parents. Making certain that a future generation is ready to support and contribute to school success is worth the effort.

A few key moves make parent communication effective now and greatly influence the future effectiveness of schools. Head off issues before they become too big, follow effective listening practices, and provide adequate professional development so that everyone knows how to deal positively with parents and other members of the public.

Making parents part of the student's total successful educational experience only makes sense. Your reputation as an effective leader is measured in part by how you communicate with parents and create solutions and learning on behalf of your students. This leadership at the classroom, office, school, and central office helps form community opinion and influences the course of education in your community. Seek the strategies and methods that create a positive culture with a focus on learning and growing students who are ready to take on the future.

FURTHER READINGS

Breakstone, S., Dreiblatt, M., & Dreiblatt, K. (2009). *How to stop bullying and social aggression.* Thousand Oaks, CA: Corwin.

Brunner, J., & Lewis, D. (2009). *Safe & secure schools.* Thousand Oaks, CA: Corwin.

Trolley, B., & Hanel, C. (2003). *Cyber kids, cyber bullying, cyber balance.* Thousand Oaks, CA: Corwin.

Wessler, S. (2003). *The respectful school.* Alexandria, VA: Association for Supervision and Curriculum Development.

CHAPTER EIGHT

RAISING THE VILLAGE BY BRINGING COMMUNITIES AND SCHOOLS TOGETHER

PAUL D. HOUSTON

I first met Bill Milliken, the founder of Communities in Schools, at a lunch that had been arranged for us by someone who thought we might be kindred spirits. Bill talked about the need to find ways to get communities engaged with schools, because the social safety net that kids need had become unraveled and schools were being asked to serve as father, mother, nurse, social worker, and priest to the children in their care.

As we ate lunch, and Bill shared with me his passionate feelings about this important topic, I told him he had come to the right place, because I thought we needed to get schools into communities! That said, we forged a bond and began working to make both things happen. The key to student success in our fractured world is to find ways to get the community more engaged with children and

———————— ————————

The key to student success in our fractured world is to find ways to get the community more engaged with children and to get our children more engaged with the community.

to get our children more engaged with the community. The pivotal person in making all this happen is the school leader.

What I had in mind in terms of getting the school into the community was moving beyond the notion that the only place where children can be educated is in school. We need to shake off this limited thinking to enable us to see the rich opportunities that the broader community offers for real and meaningful learning experiences for children. To do that, we must become more open to the community so that these ties can be strengthened.

Meanwhile, Bill was absolutely right. The schools must find ways of bringing communities into schools by opening up the school system to more outside involvement. In the short run, this is threatening to schools because of a fear of losing control somehow. But Bill's point—that we cannot ask schools to be all things to all children—is vitally important. Schools will drown under the unreal expectations of trying to meet every single need, but they can be buoyed up by the support that groups on the outside can provide.

There is a famous African proverb that educators love to quote, made still more famous by Hillary Clinton: "It takes a village to raise a child." This sentiment strikes at the heart of the challenge for educators. The task of educating can only be done successfully if there is a "team" working to accomplish the challenge. Schools are tasked with the central mission of educating—that is why parents send their children off each morning. But education does not take place in a vacuum. If the child is sick, or abused, or ill-prepared, the school is rolling the boulder uphill in trying to overcome these core issues. It takes parents and the broader community to help prepare the whole child. In today's world, unfortunately, those elements of wider support are often missing. So when educators want to quote that handy proverb, they need to ask a follow-up question—"What does it take to raise a village?"—for our children are growing up today in a world that lacks the strong web of support necessary to ensure life success.

What is the lesson here for leaders? It is that the first task of a school is to shoulder the task of remaking the village. This is the only way real success is possible. Schools exist at the physical and psychological center of communities. Walk through most communities and it won't take you long to find a school. This "centeredness" of the school came about for historical reasons, but it prevails to this day. So schools have long been at the physical center of communities, and they have also occupied the social and psychological center. Though our society has changed dramatically, the school still stands, and it could be used as a magnet for creating a more vibrant "village." But schools have often not taken full advantage of their central location. Historically, educators have viewed their work as *their* work and kept the community at arm's length. That state of affairs has begun to change, but most schools are still not using their centrality as a means of creating a stronger community.

Schools and those working in them must open themselves to the broader community. First, we must make schools more "parent friendly." School leaders should do periodic checks on how "friendly" they are. In today's post-Columbine world, schools have, of necessity, closed in to protect children from possible harm, but some have been able to do this without creating a fortress-like environment. We should not make our schools into places that give parents the feeling that they are going for visitation, or that we are fearful of their "breaking in" to break *out* their children.

At the same time, we need to work with parents to help them support a learning environment for their children. We know from research that parents are their children's first and most important teachers. We can support that important role through offering parent academies and classes on how they can help their children. Giving especially low-income parents this awareness, and showing what they can do to help their children, could have a significant impact on later achievement. Without such heightened awareness, we simply cannot expect that children who have had 4 or 5 years of limited language development will be successful in school. But we can begin to intervene in those first 5 years to start to change the arc of their lives by helping their parents do a great job as their child's first teacher. To do so requires that schools rethink their organization and philosophy to make certain that parents occupy a central place.

Engaging parents is not enough, however. Schools must find ways of getting the whole community involved. In most communities these days, only about 30 percent of the population have children in school. The rest have either already raised their children or do not have children. This is a critical point for schools as they try to pass budgets or bond issues. The attitude in the community is often either,

"It's not my problem" or "I raised my kids and now it's someone else's problem." Therefore, if for no other reason than the most practical, schools must reach out to the community. But the community can play a much larger part—they can help educate children.

The creation of volunteer and tutoring programs can draw on this valuable community resource. Study after study shows that when children feel *connected,* they do better. Being connected to a caring adult can make all the difference for many children. A core human need is to have a sense of purpose. Making it easy for members of the community to contribute to the future of children is a very powerful purpose, and it gives the children—many of whom come from homes where support is often not available—the scaffolding to grow stronger. This can be done through volunteer mentoring programs or by simply welcoming the community into school activities.

One key way to involve the community with school is through the creation of "community schools." These are places that not only offer courses to the community, but bring in the resources of the community to serve the children. When I worked in Riverside, California, one of our schools included a clinic where doctors and dentists made regular visits to the school to service the children, as well as any low-income parents who needed help. This same school also housed resident social workers from some community organizations who found it much easier to gain access to students and their families by being in the school rather than trying to get people to come to their offices. We even had a branch of the welfare office there so parents didn't have to go downtown to get assistance. New York City has had a long-standing relationship with the Children's Aid Society, which has done great work in bringing support resources from the community into the school. My point is that there are many ways to link communities and schools, but it has to start with a sense of openness from the school to get things moving.

Another major way in which schools can work with the community is in the area of after-school activities. Not only should school facilities be made available to the community, but the community can also support the needs of the school in the after-school area. In Princeton, New Jersey, after we were able to pass a bond issue to upgrade our athletic facilities, we welcomed community use of them when they were not being used by students. It was quite common to see citizens playing ball on our fields and jogging on our track. And it made the next bond issue a lot easier to pass, because members of the community saw that they benefited, too.

In any community, there are nonprofit organizations that provide after-school programs and care for children. Giving such organizations access to school facilities opens up possibilities for them and makes it easier on the children. You can also provide a much broader array of enrichment activities by inviting community members to share their expertise with students. We had mothers—many of whom had no formal education, but who could cook like a dream or do creative crafts or carpentry—leading classes on those things they were good at. In the low-income areas, this had the added bonus of letting parents and students know that we valued what they and their families were bringing to the school.

To do any of this "village raising" requires a new attitude from school leaders. I have often suggested that we should stop talking about "superintendents of schools" or "principals of schools" and start talking about superintendents or principals of *learning.* Schooling is not about the *place,* as an isolated venue, but about the processes and the relationships that lead to learning.

> *Schooling is not about the* place, *as an isolated venue, but about the processes and the relationships that lead to learning.*

I'd like to see leaders worry less about the "Killer B's" of leadership—buildings, buses, books, bonds, and so forth—and begin to master the Four C's: communication, community building, collaboration, and connection. School leadership today is about understanding that learning is a 24/7 proposition. The school plays an important role as facilitator of learning, but to truly make a difference in the lives of children, the whole 360 degrees of their existence must be taken into consideration.

Getting children truly ready for school means

- Starting to think about what needs to happen at the prenatal level, and how the schools might have an impact on the lives of expectant parents.
- Finding ways to see that children's health needs are met while they are toddlers, and what the school can do to facilitate that.
- Finding ways to help parents learn to parent effectively.

Getting children ready for school means—in the ways I just outlined and many more—finding ways of bringing the school and community together to make a difference in the lives of children. We know that much of children's critical learning takes place well before they get to school. We must find ways of intervening in those years so that positive results can ensue. We know also that about 90 percent of every child's life is spent outside of school, so we have to create ways of working with parents and the community to see that those hours are not wasted. School leaders need to start focusing on how to "raise the entire village," so the future of our children can be assured.

INDEX

CORWIN PRESS

The Corwin logo—a raven striding across an open book—represents the union of courage and learning. Corwin is committed to improving education for all learners by publishing books and other professional development resources for those serving the field of PreK–12 education. By providing practical, hands-on materials, Corwin continues to carry out the promise of its motto: **"Helping Educators Do Their Work Better."**

The HOPE Foundation logo stands for Harnessing Optimism and Potential Through Education. TheHOPE Foundation helps to develop and support educational leaders over time at district- and state-widelevels to create school cultures that sustain all students'achievement,especially low-performing students.

American Association of School Administrators

The American Association of School Administrators, founded in 1865, is the professional organization for over 13,000 educational leaders across America. AASA's mission is to support and develop effective school system leaders who are dedicated to the highest qualitypublic education for all children.